The Peases

and the

'S&D Railway'

By

Bernard McCormick

Above 'Masons Arms', of the day; where the Railway began :'

ISBN 978-0-9541756-9-6.

Typeset in 11pt Times New Roman
Titles in 22pt Eurostar
Typesetting and originating by
Bermac Publications.
bmccormick@bermac.co.uk
01325-318551

Printed and Bound in Great Britain

BY MACDONALD PRESS LIMITED, TUDHOE.

Cover photograph used with kind permission of Locomotion:
The National Railway Museum at Shildon
Cover design: www.apostledesigns.co.uk

10199026 (Opening of the S&D Railway:)
10247295 (Pictorial Collection 1825)
10419829 (Blenkinsop Train 1825)
10324771 (Remains of Stephenson's Rocket 1876)
10253866 (Stephenson's Colliery Loco 1824)
10301008 (Planet Locomotive)
The above images by: kind permission of
National Museum of Science & Industry

BIBLIOGRAPHY

Victoria History of the Counties of England	William Page
History of Durham Vol 2	William Page
Timothy Hackworth & the Locomotive	Robert Young
Exploring Local History	James Griffen
Great Engineers	J.F. Layson
History of Durham vol 1	Robert Surtees
History of Durham vol 2	Robert Surtees
Great Men of Durham	L. Cooper
Dared & Done	Julia Markus
Great Engineers	J.F. Layson
A Wealth of Happiness and Journals of	Sir Edward Pease
Many Bitter Trials (a Restless Man)	
Historical Outline of the Association of	Edward Pease
(born1799- 1872)	
Men of Business and Politics	M.W. Kirby
The Birth of the Modern	Paul Johnson
Durham	Arthur Mee
History of the Stockton Darlington Railway	J.S. Jeans
Diaries of Edward Pease Edited by	A.E.Pease

Many years ago Frank Graham Published a short version of the S&D Railway, the S&D Railway maps were first class and well laid out. I wrote to Frank for permission to re-produce the maps. Sometime later Richard Graham his son contacted me saying that Frank had sadly died, but he informed me kindly that I could use Frank's layout maps and any other graphics that I needed to make my version as accurate as possible. The maps were laid out mainly in time for the 1975 celebrations and there are some references to that period:

(Some Photographs of Shildon by the Author)

Train entering Shildon tunnel fully loaded with coal:

For Darren & Jayne

PREFACE

The S & D Railway was officially opened September 1825, the rest of the North of England if not the whole Country & even the world watched with interest. The Peases played a major role in Establishing this exciting rail venture and infact it was the first passenger travelling railway in the world. George Stephenson was chief engineer and I have charted this brilliant time in history having a look at all of the people involved along the way. Through trials and tribulations to the final successful conclusion. I have also followed the Route and noted the progress of every individual section.

The man credited to pushing this project forward was undoubtedly Edward Pease; he found cash and resources when all else had failed. I have also added selected years of the Edward Pease Diaries to the end of the story and this makes compelling reading; he shares with the public his innermost thoughts and later his sadness when losing his great friend and wife Rachel, & his grandson John Henry in 1854, then on to his final sad death in July 1858. The diaries were made public some years ago, edited by A.E. Pease, but are long out of print and I have again made selected years available to the public. In the Diaries the years 1840 & 1843 mention the death's of Jonathan Backhouse & George Stephenson; also in 1851 the discovery of a large amount of Iron Ore in the Cleveland hills.

Edward, found the balance of £7000, which was needed to progress the legislation for the S&D Railways when all else had failed; saving years of delay in the Companies second application. Edward also backed the Stephenson's in their engineering works at Forth Street, Newcastle enabling them to produce the brilliant Locomotives that was the start of a wonderful transport system throughout the world. Joseph, Edward's second son put an equal amount of work into coal and collieries, owning many in the North of England transporting the coal on the family owned railways. The family also showed that they could work hand in hand with the miners in adversity at the sad time of strikes and recession.

Throughout the trials and tribulations of the S&D, George & Robert Stephenson kept producing the best Locomotives in the world & exported them world wide, they made profit when the Peases were hit by heavy recession and the dividends from the Company kept them going to the brilliant conclusion of the S&D Railway Company; later Robert produced the best bridges known to man. Edward Pease initially sponsored the Stephenson's after the famous meeting at Darlington. I have told the story of this & the wonderful people in history that created the wealth of the period for the benefit of *all.*

Coal Every worthwhile invention over this period was developed around the power of the age '**Coal**' as the S&D became more and more established production increased enormously all over the North of England and I have included people who I felt was very important in producing this wonderful power of the day.

At the time of the 'Ironstone Boom' in Middlesbrough, Joseph and the family backed 'Bolckow & Vaughan', in their quest to develop the ironstone from the Cleveland Hills, also converting their own coal operation into coke to support the production of iron. They even had bailiffs removed from Bolckow & Vaughan sites when the partners had cash flow problems. Advice came from the family on the re-structure of Middlesbrough to make it into a thriving port.

Although Darlington benefited from Libraries, Alms Houses, Market Halls, Market areas, Cemeteries, most of the North of England were grateful for Miner's Hospitals and Schools, Mechanics and Miner's Institutes, Assembly Rooms', But the family can be remembered mainly for their part played in the early Railways.

Locomotion the first engine to transport fare paying passengers, the train also carried coal from Peases 'Witton Park Colliery', like Etherly Coal it was quality coal supplying the Royal Palaces in London:

The Peases

Early years from 1665

Joseph Pease was born in 1665, descended from Landowners in Essex in the 15th century – one of whom settled at Sikehouse, South Yorkshire, in the reign of Henry VIII. By the end of the 17th century, Joseph was well established as a Landowner at Pease Hall, Shafton Green, Felkirk, in the West Riding.

In 1706, Joseph married Ann Caldwell, heiress to her brother's business as wool combers and merchants. Out of this wedlock came 3 sons and 2 daughters and it was the second son, Edward, who would progress this story, and be of most interest to Darlington and the North of England. Edward's father died when he was 8 years old, in 1719, leaving him with strong Quaker stock traditions, his mother also came from a similar background. In 1735 Edward married Elizabeth Coates, also a Quaker, from Caselee and Langley Ford, in Co. Durham. The marriage took place at Raby Meeting House, near Darlington; Edward was by now, a member of The 'Society of Friends'. Edward's status at this time was very vague, his elder brother had inherited the property at Felkirk, and Edward entered the wool business with his uncle, Thomas Cauldwell, who retired in 1760. Edward took over the business, offering his brother George a job, (George was a non Quaker, who when joining the army in 1740 fought at Culloden). So the foundations of the Pease Dynasty were laid. Thomas Cauldwell of Darlington (wife's family) being the start of the Pease family fortunes. It was halfway through the 18th Century that Darlington was quickly establishing itself as a prominent market town, only second to Durham, in importance. Darlington district was rich in farming communities, especially in the vale of the Tees. In the early years, the population was approximately 3,300 inhabitants – who were more or less dependent on manufacturing created by agriculture; the woollen and worsted industries and also the manufacture of linen and the Tanning Industry.

In 1790, the Peases were the most important producer of Linen, supplying yarns for manufacturers in Durham, Yorkshire and Cumberland. Wool also grew in importance, and just prior to the start of the Industrial Revolution, they were Britain's most important manufacturer. From the date Edward Pease took over there was a marked improvement in all aspects of the wool trade, especially in weaving and dyeing. The mill was situated at Priestgate, near the River Skerne; they also had a smaller mill at Leadyard.

The mills generated years of uninterrupted work even to the present century, at one time employing 700 workers, buying wool from farmers, sorting it, giving it to the cottages to be combed. The wool was then spun and then sold. The money made from this industry enabled the Peases to come through many difficult periods, and without the revenue from the wool they would not have survived. Edward died in 1785, leaving a will, which was made shortly before his death. His estate left tenements, dwelling houses, shops, warehouses, and workhouses, to be equally divided between 5 sons, and 2 daughters, the silver plate was shared between all of his children equally. Each son was to receive the contents of 1 room, while the daughters shared the Delftware and the china. The value of these legacies was £3900, but the main benefactor was Joseph, who was the main successor to the woollen business.

Around about 1785 the Woollen Business was known as Joseph Pease and Sons, at this time he also branched into banking, in a moderate way; this was known as Pease Partners Bank. In the years between 1765-99 the Bank held 109 accounts paying an interest rate of 4.5% annually. Some accounts were held for the Pease family, but the majority of the accounts were held for people scattered in villages, throughout North Yorkshire and South West Durham. Joseph Pease was on his way.

Joseph was able to manipulate, for the banks benefit, both customers for wool, advancing them credit, and at the same time accept funds on behalf of suppliers. So no matter what stage the wool trade, the bank made money and he easily expanded the woollen side of the Pease Woollen business. Joseph's youngest sister married Jonathan Backhouse, who was founder of the banking firm J.J. Backhouse, and established at the time the Royal Exchange Insurance Company, this alliance between the Peases and the Backhouse Banking, proved very important several years ahead.

James Backhouse,

Jonathan's father James was a native of Lancaster; it seemed it was his destiny to cross the Pennines in 1746. In a matter of a few years he financed the start of the railways in the north of England. This project was the most exciting period ever known in England. James was twenty-eight and the very first year of his arrival he fell madly in love with a young lady called Jane Hedley; she was twenty eight and heiress to her fathers linen business. At the time of James' arrival at Darlington there were only 450 inhabitants but it was thriving; Darlington was well known at the time not only in England but also in the world tablecloths, napkins and other items these were sold in London and other large towns. James Backhouse was a travelling yarn dealer at the time and came into much contact with Jonathon Hedley, Jane's father and this is when they met; Hedley had premises near to the market place Darlington and his business was thriving. There was another reason why the young couple came together and that was their religion they were both Quakers and both parents wanted their offspring to marry in the faith.

James Backhouse married his fiancée Jane and began to work for her father, within a year their first child was born, who they called Jonathan, after Jane's father; a second child was born ten years later called James. James (senior) quickly established himself amongst the Darlington Quakers and often travelled to London to sell linen. James combined business with religion and often banked money in Quaker banks in London on behalf of other Quakers as well as for his business. James was soon writing letters of credit and signing bank notes for the Quakers and he eventually opened a bank in Darlington with his older son. By now, James Backhouse was prosperous and on the retirement of Jonathan Hedley, James took over his business which greatly increased his wealth and this is when he built West Lodge, Woodland Road, one of the first of many large Quaker houses in Darlington. This was the period that brought together two powerful Darlington families the Peases and the Backhouses; the Peases had came from the same district and like the Backhouses were drawn to the area because of linen production. The family were in the wool combing trade and were also on the road to a vast fortune.

Young Jonathan and Anne Pease met fell in love and married, this was a complete Quaker wedding and it was said to be a match made in heaven. At this time both the Peases and the Backhouses were members of The Society of Friends, this was a close-knit sect who not unlike the monopoly of credit established in the Lancashire cotton mills around about 1780, the only difference with the Peases, circle of business friends, this was world-wide, even in North America. The strength of the credit and banking section was re-enforced by inter marriage, and this happened

Darlington 1830

Darlington 1843

mostly in the Iron and Textile, business and banking. Not all of the Society of Friends were capitalists, and profiteers, there were quite a number of ordinary farmers, shopkeepers, craftsmen and manufacturers; all were under the protective umbrella of Joseph Pease and his associates, they were very loyal to these people who had very rich businesses. At the end of the day it was a fantastic structure of commercial enterprise, when members in difficulties, could and were, helped out by numerous strong business friends. In the early days customers handed over gold deposited at the bank; in a short time they were exchanging bank notes whenever they needed to purchase anything. Sometimes, in the early days, there was doubt whether the bank could cover the note with gold. In 1778 a forger copied Backhouse notes including the watermark, this was a great cause for concern and customers began to loose confidence.

Backhouse said that only two bank notes were in circulation, one had been passed in Sunderland, the other in Durham when muslin had been purchased. The Backhouses offered a reward of one hundred pounds for information leading to the arrest of the forger. In September 1778 they had the name of the forger who was John Mathieson of Gretna Green. He was thirty years of age, thin but strong and wiry he had a pocked face, which may have been caused by smallpox, and one leg was thicker than the other and may have been broken at one time. His description was circulated in the press, he also apparently had a Scottish accent and believed to be hiding somewhere in Durham or Newcastle. Mathieson found his cover blown and headed for London, where he began forging Bank of England notes after changing his name to Maxwell. He was arrested in 1779 when he denied all knowledge of forging notes, but after the Constable produced his description from the Backhouses he finally broke down and confessed; he offered to tell how he forged notes with the watermarks in return for his freedom.

This was refused and Mathieson was tried convicted and hanged at Newgate Prison on July 28th 1779. While the Backhouse bank was rid of the forger, the possibility of fraud was installed in the minds of people and there were runs on the bank in the years 1793,1797,1815. Customers flocked to the bank demanding gold for their bank notes; the Backhouses survived mainly because of the loyalty of their friends like the Pease family and other Quakers. One man who was exceptionally useful to the bank at the time was Thomas Ord of Newton, who was actually Archdeacon of North West Darlington. He campaigned among rich and influential farmers, driving in his carriage to outlying farmers

Above Jonathan Backhouse of Polam Hall, started serious banking at Darlington, the premises now Barclays

persuading them to back the Backhouse bank; he even posted leaflets everywhere in Darlington on the Sunday prior to the bank opening on the Monday morning Backhouse survived but others were less fortunate. Mowbray & Hollingsworth and Company, who also had a bank at Durham, collapsed. The Backhouses took advantage of the misfortune and opened a bank at Durham. The collapsed bank also left premises in the High Row, Darlington and the Backhouses moved in from Northgate, which was situated some way from the heart of real business; Barclays Bank, to this day occupy this building. It was generally thought that without the help of Thomas Ord the Backhouses would not have survived. Jonathan Backhouse, as a further precaution, made trips to London where he collected his gold, he would return to the Darlington Bank. He did this quite casually leaving in his top hat rather unconcerned, then proceeding to Scotch Corner Inn, on the Great North Road, where a coach and four horses waited for him to travel to the capital. This was the procedure he carried out in case there was an increased demand to cash bank notes at the bank.

The Father of the Railways (Edward Pease)

Joseph Pease died in 1808. Although the woollen trade was very profitable, they still had a long way to go before they could compare themselves with Lloyds, Barclays, Bevans, and the Gurneys, and in the year 1796 the spinning of worsted yarn commenced. Although banking was still progressing on a small scale, trading had spread to Scotland, and the West of England, the main line of thought in those days, up to the year 1800, was the conveyance of inland coal, to a navigable point, on the River Tees. The man who completed this task was Edward, Joseph's eldest son; he would be very much involved in the furtherance of the coal

Darlington Business men gave notice that they had full confidence in the Backhouse Bank in the light of many Bank Failures: Below Cast Iron Bridge at Yarm.

Darlington Bank.

WE, the undersigned Inhabitants of DARLINGTON, assure the Country, that we continue to feel the most entire Confidence in the BANK of *Jonathan Backhouse & Co.*, and that we take and pay their Notes as usual.

DARLINGTON,

Monday, 8th July, 1810.

Backhouse Bank, High Row, Darlington (1815-1864), in the present day 'Barclays Bank'. below a Five Pound note from the Backhouse Bank at the time:

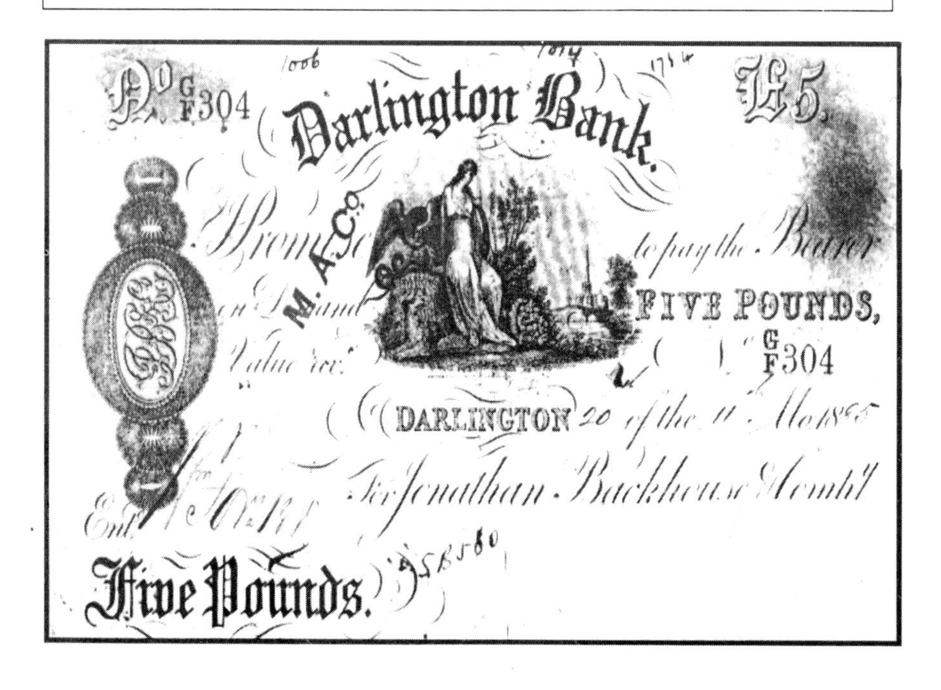

Peases Mill, Priestgate founded 1752, The family employed many of the Darlington people, even though at times work was short they still kept the workforce employed. Below The Three Arch Bridge which was built in 1767:

industry, and the development of the railways.

The Peases & The S&D Railway

Edward was born in 1767 and, after attending schools in Darlington, at the age of 11 was sent to the Quaker boarding school of Joseph and Sarah Tatham at Leeds, returning back to Darlington at the age of 14. He was a typical product of 18th Century schooling, educated in English, proficient in French and able to paint and draw a little. He was extremely numerate, as later ledgers showed, and by the time he was 18 he was very acquainted with business; he travelled from place to place buying and selling – and doing this very well. Edward was said to be the 'Father of the Railways' and writers of the time, such as Samuel Smiles, went even further saying he was a man who could see a hundred years ahead; although he was a good supporter of the railways, his foresight did not go far beyond this, and it was his son, Joseph, who pushed the Pease Dynasty into the Railway and Coal Industry.

Edward Pease was fully behind the anti-Slave bill that was being introduced at the time and he campaigned strongly for it. He was not what one could call a fully-fledged Quaker. Edward, by 1817, was still very much a part of the woollen industry, and he was also acclaimed as the railway pioneer. He was now in his fifties, and the Society of Friends were getting more of his attention. He continued to campaign relentlessly for the Anti-Slave bill. At about this time he suffered a very disastrous fire at the Woollen Mill at Priestgate, Darlington.

The River Tees was found not adequate as a navigable river, For the transport of goods and in 1767 a group of 153 promoters, among them being the Peases and Backhouses, agreed to fund a survey for a canal. It was carried out by Robert Whitworth, acting for James Brindley. The route proposed being Stockton by Darlington to a point on the northbank of the Tees at Winston and within easy reach of the South Durham Mines. Total length of the canal being 33 miles, at a cost of £63,722. The project was very adventurous for the lightly populated area of the times and the scheme was abandoned due to the lack of public interest.

There was renewed interest in 1790, then further interest in 1810, when a channel shortened the distance from the mouth of the Tees to Stockton by 2 miles and was called the Mandale scheme. A dinner was held at Stockton to celebrate. Leonard Raisbeck the recorder of Stockton, used the occasion to inaugurate a project for the construction of a Canal or a Railroad for the transportation of coals and other minerals. The Pease family were very interested; the original Winston scheme was again put forward by John Rennie but was again abandoned in 1815, in the aftermath of many bank failures in County Durham.

Around about the year 1814 the Peases acquired an interest in a colliery at Witton, near Bishop Auckland, and this would have a very big influence on the opening of the Stockton Darlington Railway, in 1825. At the start of 18th Century coal was the most important national product, and mines were being sunk as fast as sinkers could be found to sink them. William Coulson, the celebrated Master Sinker of the times, had sunk over 100 shafts up to 1865. Coulson was the Master Sinker, who some years later, with his son and other sinkers, tried in vain to free entombed miners at Hartley Colliery in 1862. All landowners lived in the hope of finding, coal, iron, copper, or lead on their land.

Christopher Tennant was a leading merchant in Stockton, who put forward a very revolutionary scheme and funded his own survey. The scheme was for a canal route to the Auckland coalfield via. Rushyford and well to the north of Darlington. There were many anomalies to such a project; one being it would require 50 locks and the engineering problems were immense. Later it was known to be a sound commercial proposition; it came further north than Darlington and was indeed a shorter route to the coalfields. Tennant also hoped to get further coal trade from the coast areas. The construction cost of the scheme was £205,283 and was endorsed at a public meeting held in Stockton in July 1818.

Tennant led a deputation to London hoping to raise the money; four fifths was required for the construction after which the parliamentary authorization would be forthcoming. At this time the Yarm/Darlington supporters were livid and immediately put forward a rival scheme, this time including Piercebridge, as well as Croft and Yarm, with a tramway or railroad from this point to the Collieries. George Coverton, a Welsh engineer, took on the job he had considerable experience of laying rail in Wales, he was also a relative of a Yarm promoter, who was engaged as surveyor. His report was put forward on September 18th.1818

The report came out strongly in support of a continuous line of Railway of 27 miles at a cost of £124,000, rejecting the canal schemes out of hand, and this proved the most economical and most efficient scheme, and Edward Pease's views were vindicated. At a meeting held on Friday 13th November at Darlington Town Hall to consider Overton's report. Backhouse made a strong and effective speech in favour of the Railroad Project and demolished any further backing for the Tennant went on further to say 5% profit was the minimum return on outlay and it was very probable that up to 12% could be made, but Edward said that he would be quite content with his 5% anything over and above was sheer profit, with that the meeting ended.

Burnhopeside Hall, near Lanchester later the residence of William Hedley pictured below:

Scheme, for the canal via Rushy-ford. Backhouse went on to promise a return of 25% on £120,000. Backhouse appeared over enthusiastic and it was left to Edward Pease to install a little common sense back into the proceedings. He dashed present calculations on the present railway figures saying that a railroad was assured a positive 5% return. Edward

William Hedley

William Hedley was very much at the fore of early steam power discoveries in the North of England Later Hedley made many experiments with Locomotives and produced '*Puffing Billy*' and '*Wylam Dilly*' tired of experimentation he finally bought a Locomotive from R & W. Hawthorn. William Hedley appealed against George Stephenson being classed as the 'Father of the Railways', putting forward Evidence of the 'Wylam Trials'; He was well known as one of the original **'Grand**

Chaldron Wagons as they were in 1773 just were not adequate for the growing demand for coal and its by-products; in the background a keel can be seen. John Blenkinsop and his associates were aware of Trevithicks work on steam engines and they developed an engine at Middleton Railway, Manchester in 1812, seen below which revolutionised coal haulage: Middleton Colliery Railway, opened in 1812, It was seen passing Christ's Church, Leeds the brainchild of John Blenkinsop who progressed Trevithicks original idea for locomotives:

Allies', this claim was the last registered by Hedley on the subject. Later he took on the lease of 'Crowtrees Colliery', Bowburn in 1835 & after five years Hedley decided to sell up later he moved to Lanchester where he purchased Burnhopside Hall, still having many mining interests.

Wylam became the main centre for experimentation; Hedley as viewer at Wylam Colliery must have been highly experienced in mechanics at least to the same level as Hackworth. In 1802 Trevithick had patented his engine, which he had tested in Wales & in the following years his locomotive ideas were being closely scrutinized especially at Wylam, Northumberland. There were people here that were fully devoted to producing a steam engine to haul coal from the inland collieries to coastal ports. All of this group of men were convinced that the way forward in the industry was in fact steam engines, and not horse or canal transport which would be essential to push forward our natural power and product.

The dream became a reality when the group began experimenting on Locomotives these men were George Stephenson, Christopher Blackett (owner of the Colliery), William Hedley, (Colliery Viewer), Timothy Hackworth (Foreman Blacksmith), and Jonathan Foster (Millwright). Tom Waters built a test engine, similar to Trevithick's which was being closely scrutinized; it had a 6-inch cylinder and single through fire flue. The engine came through initial tests with flying colours. There was also another man taking in all of the proceeding's at this time he was Robert Hawthorn of Walbottle, *in a short period he would be known as 'R. & W. Hawthorn' (famous engine builders).*

All were absolutely sure and convinced that steam power was the way forward. However the main enthusiasm for the project came from Christopher Blackett. Blackett was passionately interested in Trevithick's invention some years previously when Hackworth was an apprentice and before Hedley was employed at Wylam, it was Blackett that had arranged further experiments.

John Blenkinsop of Middleton who was a Colliery Viewer and part owner of the Colliery patented his steam engine on April 10th. 1811 no 3431. This led to the famous experiment on June 24th. 1812, when his Steam Engine conveyed coals from mines at Middleton to Leeds at 10 MPH. There were 8 loaded coal wagons at which the 'Leeds Mercury', gave a good report. But basically the most important experiments were happening at Wylam.

George Stephenson (early)

George Stephenson was employed at Killingworth Colliery; his work as an Engine man was impressive in 1814; he was also a great friend of Jonathan Foster the Wylam Engine Wright. This is where Stephenson gained all the experience required to drive his dream forward.

Saturday afternoons was the period when Stephenson learnt most while others were at leisure. Another man accompanied Stephenson at this time his name was Nicholas Wood, he was viewer at Killingworth Colliery. George Stephenson had a great gift of self-confidence. He was certain that he could improve on Blenkinsops engine mainly with the knowledge gained from Wylam and he fully intended to push his ideas forward. With the knowledge gained by Stephenson the owners of Killingworth Colliery & the 'Grand Allies', decided to build a Locomotive. This was '*Blucher*'; built 1814 it was a mixture of Wylam and Blenkinsop's Locomotive. It took George Stephenson ten months', to build "*Blucher*" & when completed it was tested on the Cillingwood Railway on July 25, 1814. The track was uphill of four hundred and fifty feet. George Stephenson's engine hauled eight loaded coal wagons weighing thirty tons, at about four miles an hour. This was the first steam engined powered locomotive to run on a railroad and it was the most successful working steam engine that had ever been constructed up to this period, this encouraged the inventor to make further experiments. In all, Stephenson built sixteen different engines. In 1822 Stephenson further developed Locomotives using Hetton for a base and for experimentation. George Stephenson's civil Engineering skills together with his brilliant self tought ability to survey was also unique and his services were required all over the Country and as more Collieries were sunk he was required even more.

All of the Grand Allies were convinced that steam Locomotives were the way forward, but they gradually all went their own way's. Timothy Hackworth at the age of 27 married Jane Golightly at Ovingham Parish Church. She was a tall well-educated handsome woman who fitted perfectly to Hackworth's world. They started a family while they were still based at Wylam. Hackworth and his wife were devout Methodists and Lay preachers; because he would not break the Sabbath refraining from working on that day he had to part with his employers at Wylam one of these being William Hedley. Early 1816 Hackworth was offered the position of Foreman Black Smith at Walbottle Colliery. He accepted the position when from that day Wylam ceased to be the activity Colliery for Locomotive tests.

Francis Mewburn above was a powerful man as 'Chief Bailiff':

Francis Mewburn

Mewburn was born at Bishop Middleham in 1785, he was said *to be the legal brains behind the S&D Railway. He was also credited to being 'Chief Bailiff', of Darlington which was a Mayoral position and which ceased on his death in 1867.*

Mewburn and Raisbeck were joint Solicitors on the S&D project, but in 1828 Raisbeck resigned. Mewburn was not flattered by a remark made by Joseph Pease, when he told him he had the heart of a chicken; his family motto was *'Festina Lente',* hasten with caution. Mewburn attended school at Ormsby near Middlesbrough, then later he was articled to a solicitor at Durham; he moved to Darlington in 1809 and it was here he began his law business. He married the daughter of Mr. Smales, Elizabeth, in 1813; they had a rather large family of girls and lived in a large house at the junction of Larchfield Street, and Coniscliffe Road, Darlington.

St. Augustine's Church Hall is on this location in the present day. The house was originally owned by the Backhouse family and named by them '*Paradise*', this was quickly changed by Mewburn. By the time the railway was progressing, in 1818, his solicitor practice was flourishing; this was when the population was around 5000. Francis attended St. Cuthbert's Church, his family not being Quakers, and in the present day a window is dedicated in his honour. This window features St. Andrew and St. Barnabas; he was born and died on their feast days. For all he was not a Quaker he was chosen to assist Edward Pease and Jonathan Backhouse in the litigation leading to the birth of the S&D Railway. He also attended 'The Holy Trinity Church', in Woodland road and here again there is a plaque erected in his honour.

As stated, Mewburn became Chief Bailiff of Darlington being the Bishop of Durham's, representative. In 1846 Mewburn died of Bright's disease, (kidney disease). The position of Bailiff ceased when Darlington became a Borough in 1868. Mewburn performed many duties one being the laying of the foundation stone for Skerne Bridge, in 1824 (*on the back of a £5 note*). He also started the Blackwell Bridge, in 1832. Mewburn was best known however for the legalities of the S&D Railways, he attended dinners and many functions to promote the S&D system. He predicted that Darlington people would be able to leave Darlington any morning attend an opera at London in the evening and be home again by breakfast time, but breakfast should have read tea-time.

Inaugural Meeting S&D Railway

The well-attended inaugural meeting concluded, and the people, having full confidence in these respectable people, appointed a 40 strong management committee, made up from those prepared to subscribe £500 to the project.

The prospectus was devised by no other than Joseph Pease, who was then only 19 years of age. It was issued on the 15th Nov. 1818, and within 1 week £25,000 had been easily raised. The subscription list had to be closed on 26th of December 1818 and of the 1209 shares of £100 each, the majority were local. A list of the shareholders was as follows: Backhouse Family, £20,000, Pease Family, £6,200, Quaker Benjamin Flounders of Yarm £5,000, Colonel William Chayter of Croft, £5000, Thomas Maynell of Yarm £3000, Leonard Raisbeck (*one of a few from Stockton)* £1000, there was also a great deal of outside money, mainly from the Society of Friends. The Gurney family of Norwich and London subscribed, £20,000, Thomas Richardson, of London,£10,000.When subscribers were checked, Quakers and the Society of Friends mainly financed the project.

People like the Gurneys and Thomas Richardson, showed complete confidence in these people and their Darlington cousins, Pease and Backhouse. Even if Tennant had managed to get his plan off the ground it would have been a non-starter, competing against these shareholders, who had such close ties, and kinship, and also trust. With the founders, especially the Pease, & Backhouse families. The necessary legislation was settled in Parliament, but the scheme's main problem was the landowners, and where the railroad would run.

Leonard Raisbeck

It was credited to Raisbeck that it was basically his idea to put a railway from the coalfields to the Port of Stockton. He was present at a dinner to celebrate the opening of the 'Mandale Cut', which was a two hundred yard channel that took a loop out of

Richard Trevithick, brilliant rail pioneer who's Steam Engine invention was closely scrutinised:

the Tees at Stockton, making it better for shipping. Raisbeck, instead of backing canal transport, which he thought, would destroy Darlington and Yarm, and probably also Stockton, kept the Darlington project on the move. Even though Francis Mewburn was known as the first railway Solicitor, Raisbeck once had to go to his aid when, at the prospect of addressing the House of Commons, Mewburn froze. Mewburn was younger with less worldly experience than Raisbeck..

Raisbeck rode from Darlington to London at short notice to make the speech and so progress the project. Raisbeck's family were highly respected and Leonard was a recorder and steward to the Bishop of Durham from 1804 to 1826; he was also a Colonel in the volunteers and in 1832 he was Lord Mayor.

The two most influential landowners on the route were the Earl of Darlington (later first Duke of Cleveland) and the Earl of Eldon, at that time Lord Chancellor in Lord Liverpool's administration; both of these powerful people were against the project. It was thought that Lord Eldon was bought off; Lord Darlington stood his ground saying it was unfair and oppressive to the country, but it was generally thought that the main reason for his obsessive objection was that it would inflict damage to Fox Coverts. Over this period people were starting to experiment in the haulage of coals, as more and more mines were being sunk.

Richard Trevithick was a brilliant man and also an extremely good inventor but he also lived for a good time. He was born in a mining region of Cornwall where static steam engines were used in the mines as early as 1800. Trevithick felt sure that these engines would be able to propel themselves with the use of high-pressure steam, consequently he experimented, first of all with road engines. He had tremendous success with his first machine, after which he and his friends celebrated in a local ale house. His machine boiler began to over heat, until it reached boiling point, then with an almighty bang it scattered its machinery all over the Cornish countryside.

Trevithick carried on with his experiments and gradually added iron rails at Penydarren Tramway in South Wales; linking ironworks at Merthyr Tydfil to a canal at Abercynon in 1804. Richard did not capitalise on his earlier successes preferring the good life and merrymaking. There were others who took advantage of his earlier success and pushed forward a stage further the use of engines for the transport of coals.

George Stephenson continued his experiments and built a similar but more efficient Locomotive. Stephenson simplified the transmission of thrust to the wheels by placing the unit on top of the boiler, he also devised a system to cushion it against shocks. He improved the machine more and more and the improved machine performed better than ever and so did his fame. Orders came in from all over the country; backers also came forward, among them powerful business men from the region like the Liddell's (Ravensworth Family).

Stephenson's Cottage birth place, where he returned often to watch Hedley's engines on the 'Wylam Wagon Way', just outside of the cottage:

About this period William Coulson and his team of sinkers were in the Hetton Area putting in test borings with the intention of developing the area for the production of coal. For years it had been known that a thick band of Limestone Magnesia was evident right across the strata in the area and generally thought that no coal existed below it. William Coulson proved the theory wrong and bored into quality coal in abundance below the Limestone, after which the Hetton Collieries were sunk. Hetton Colliery was the first ever-deep pit, it was 147 fathoms (1000 feet) deep and like all of the Coulson sinkings, produced coal in abundance – and was one of the most productive pits in Durham County. Miners flocked to the Hetton area and over night the production of coal doubled.

This opened the door to the Hetton Colliery Railways in 1821 and Stephenson used Hetton for most of his experiments with Locomotives. George Stephenson planned the area railway system with precision. After Thornley was sunk, Stephenson designed the new railway from Thornley with a branch to Cassop and Ludworth. The Railway opened 23rd November 1835 and the line was completed to Haswell, en-route was Shotton Colliery, Wellfield, Castle Eden & Hesleden. This was after the completion of the Liverpool/ Manchester line. Again the production along the route of the Railway spiralled and again miners flocked to the area in large numbers

Railway Progress:

The first Stockton Darlington Railway Bill was defeated on 5/4/1819, by 106 votes to 93, and the promoters were not dismayed by the narrow defeat. They worked harder to get the bill through, the Pease family lobbied strongly for extra backing in the House of Commons.

The George & Dragon Hotel at Yarm where a meeting was held for the second attempt to push the S&D Railway through Parliament:

A further survey was carried out and it was attempted to avoid Lord Darlington's Estate, as far as possible. Lord Darlington tried every way to stop the railroad and even attempted to bankrupt the Backhouse Bank. The promoters once again renewed the Application to Parliament; this was after the death of George III in January 1820.

This had a major impact on the Pease's plans for the S&D railway. On the death of George 3rd. Parliament was dissolved just as the bill was to have its final reading; the sponsors had come a long way to get the project off the ground and they met a fortnight later in the George & Dragon public house in Yarm where they resolved to start all over again.

George Overton was again employed as surveyor and they began lobbying members of Parliament, so desperate were they to get it off the ground – they had just about every MP in their service. The survey by Overton was completed on September 1st; it was thirty-seven miles long, having five branches.

By February 1821 the bill was on its way. The first and second readings were easily passed then it progressed to the committee stage and it looked destined to easily come through. The lobbying was even more intense by the promoters, and the bill was very nearly lost again – by not complying with the rules of Parliament in that four/fifths of a public company should be available, before it passed to committee stage. By February 1821 the bill was again on its way and this time they hoped that there was no problems. The first and second readings were easily passed & it progressed to the committee stage and it looked destined to easily come through.

Francis Mewburn leafed through the pages, suddenly he gasped and was totally in shock as one section caught his legally trained eyes; he read it over again, as if it had just appeared, he gasped again. The section said that 80% of the capital supporting the

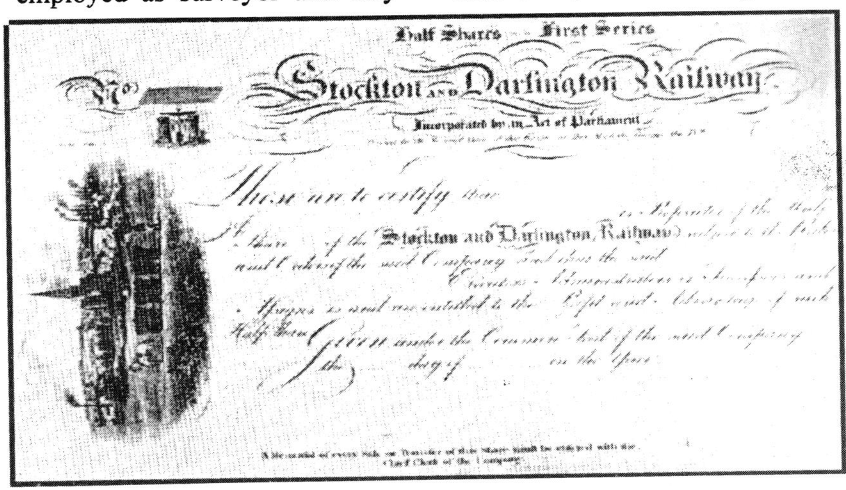
Half Shares — First Series
Stockton and Darlington Railway
Incorporated by an Act of Parliament
These are to certify that
Half Share of the Stockton and Darlington Railway
Given under the Common Seal of the said Company

S&D Share certificates; all showing a horse as the power for leading the coal:

scheme had to be forthcoming before it could progress beyond the committee stage. Later in his hotel room, Mewburn carefully checked the figures, finding that they were £7000 short of this amount; Edward Pease was informed saying they had three days to raise the capital.

Backhouse got to work with the London Quakers and Mewburn visited finance houses, desperately trying to raise the capital. They were desperate that another catastrophe would not affect their plans at this stage. The two men again met, both had negative reports and were not able to raise what was needed. Shortly before the deadline news was received that Edward Pease had produced the £7000, this was from his personnel savings and its value in the present day would be £500,000.

It was reported that Edward had no hesitation in signing the cheque for the needed amount, further strengthening his, and the Quaker, hold on the S&D Railway and giving him the tag of being *'the father of the railways'*. Every major decision came to him for approval. To the relief of all concerned, the bill progressed to the Lords on the 17th and 19th of April 1821; the Royal Assent came from George IV. Mewburn wrote the act of Parliament which was sixty-seven pages long. It provided for a Railway from the Tees to Witton Park Colliery, with branches throughout Durham; the act provided that anyone was entitled to run a wagon on it on receipt of the rate, between 7 am and 6pm in winter, and 5am and 10am in summer. Historians noted that there was no mention of coal, or for that matter steam engines, only horses and men.

One amazing fact was that there was no mention of passengers, but Locomotion No. 1 made its inaugural run on the line with mainly passengers. Over the following weeks everyone sighed with relief that they had raised the money needed from Edward Pease – with just days to spare. This also led to the resignation of Colonel Chaytor, who was the chairman of the committee, in protest to the growing dominance of Pease and Backhouse. Prior to the opening of the Railway in September 1825, Edward Pease's influence and guidance was greatly appreciated in these early days.

There was an historical meeting between Edward and George Stephenson at Darlington about this time, and Stephenson proved to have been of great help as an Engineer and guiding influence to the Peases Scheme. Thomas Maynell became Chairman of the Company, he was a Londoner and his status fitted the post. But it was Edward Pease, who was the guiding influence; he worked

The Seal of the Company showing a horse pulling the truck not a machine, the motto means 'At private risk for public service'

closely with Stephenson who at the time was Chief Engineer for them. The original railway ran from Witton Park Colliery, six miles from Bishop Auckland, and finished at a wharf on Teesside. Edward convinced himself of the practicability of the locomotive engine, devoted his life and fortune to its adoption, and perfection. In May 23rd, 1823, the first rail was laid. Edward introduced George Stephenson and his engineering genius to the world, and he also backed him. The original deed of Partnership is owned by Joseph Pease and is endorsed by Edward Pease, Robert Stephenson, Michael Longridge, and George Stephenson.

The Launch Of S&D Railway & Locomotion One

The first Locomotion completed by Robert Stephenson & Company at Forth Street works Newcastle was loaded on to three low wagons with horses, owned by a Company called Pickersgill. The engine was transported down the great north road to Aycliffe Village on the 16th September 1825. On arrival

at Aycliffe the strange procession turned right towards Heighington Village; arriving at the part of the lane where the railway rails cross the lane, this is where the wagons stopped. Eager strong men and boys helped to unload the strange machines, carefully watched by George Stephenson.

The engine was assembled on the site of the now 'Locomotion Hotel', then it was 'Heighington Station', just past the level crossing of the road; where it was placed on the rails. Locomotion was fired up within two days of its arrival; the boiler was filled with water and wood and coals were ready. No one

Above first Passenger coach:

had a light to flame the boiler and George Stephenson sent to Aycliffe for a lighted lantern. Just prior to his return, a navvy, Robert Metcalf, of Church Street, Darlington, came forward with a magnifying glass that he used to light his pipe by the sun. Stephenson used this and in a short time the boilers were just about at boiling point.

By September 26th the Locomotive was running smoothly, and on the day of the so called 'Experiment', it carried celebrities like the Pease family, headed by Edward, and sons Joseph and Henry, also their Quaker cousin Thomas Richardson. Another guest was William Kitching (he had a foundry in Tubwell Row, later he moved to Hope Town where he opened a company which was later known as Whessoe; the Company employed a high number of people from the area until well into the nineteenth century).

George Stephenson was also a passenger and his brother, James, drove the Locomotive on the day.It travelled from Aycliffe to Shildon to be coupled to the rest of the wagons that waited at Shildon and it was the first Locomotive to draw a carriage in the world. All over the north of England people waited in anticipation, for the 'Experiment'; Colliery owners, Engineers & ordinary workers knew the importance of the event.

Above 'Masons Arms', of the day; where the Railway began :'

came up to him and asked if he pulled the leavers that made the engine move. The wagons started from the '*Masons Arms*', Shildon. The carriages with the celebrities waited in anticipation; to be joined to the train where Hundreds of people clung to the sides; as a static engine pulled the wagons 1,960 yards to the top of the bank; then lowered them 880 yards down the other side, where Locomotion waited patiently, its steam at the ready. People waited in anticipation and when it did pull away most appeared frightened. It was reported that 300 people did not want tickets for the first journey but approximately 600 hitched a ride on the wagons determined to be on the trip.

The directors took their places in the experimental passenger rail car where 18 could be seated. The carriages numbered 38. Locomotion was followed by five wagons full of coal and passengers, a wagon of flour and passengers, a wagon of surveyors and engineers, 14 wagons of standing workmen, and six

The Big Day

At dawn on Tuesday September 27th, 1825, thousands of people headed towards Shildon to Witness the new railway, and Locomotion No.1. Even as early as 5.30 am, donkeys horses and mules trudged towards the railway; also at Darlington people flocked to see the amazing sight. Early that particular morning Isaac Pease breathed his last at his father's house in Northgate, Darlington; his passing would certainly be remembered on this historic day. It was said that his brothers were not at the house when he died; Edward was tremendously sad as Isaac was his favourite, and he loved him tremendously.

There was a story that Joseph was at the launch of S&D Railway; as he stood near the track watching, an old farmer

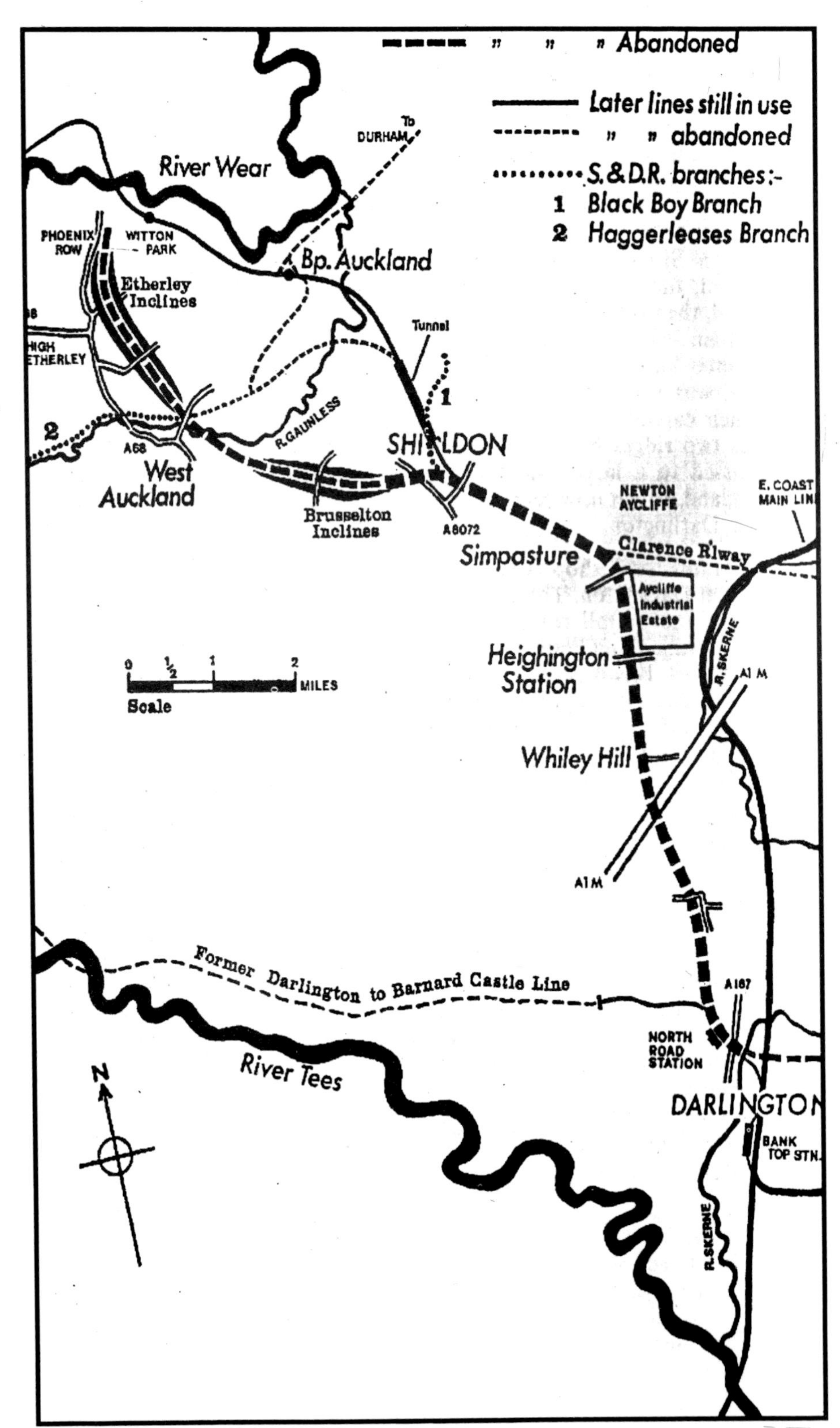
" " " Abandoned
Later lines still in use
" " abandoned
S.&D.R. branches:-
1 Black Boy Branch
2 Haggerleases Branch
To DURHAM
River Wear
PHOENIX ROW
WITTON PARK
Bp. Auckland
Etherley Inclines
HIGH ETHERLEY
Tunnel
R. GAUNLESS
1
2
A68
West Auckland
SHILDON
Brusselton Inclines
A6072
Simpasture
NEWTON AYCLIFFE
E. COAST MAIN LINE
Clarence R'lway
Aycliffe Industrial Estate
Heighington Station
R. SKERNE
A1 M
0 ½ 1 2 MILES
Scale
Whiley Hill
A1M
Former Darlington to Barnard Castle Line
A167
NORTH ROAD STATION
River Tees
N
DARLINGTON
BANK TOP STN.
R. SKERNE

The Inaugural first Journey of the S&D Railway, with Stephenson's Locomotion 1:

Dobbins Watercolour of the opening of the S&D Railway, crossing 'Bonomi's Bridge,' still in use today across the Skerne; Below the 'Suspension Bridge', designed at Middlesbrough by Captain S. Brown, to extend the travel of the S&D Railway to the Middlesbrough drops & which turned out to be a disaster as the wagons could only be handled four at a time:

wagons of coal and passengers made up the historic train. Rail workers wore blue buttonholes and the men on duty wore blue sashes, these were the men who operated the brakes in between the wagons. Timothy Hackworth acted as guard and George Stephenson's brothers Ralph & James were in charge of the engine. At 10am, Hackworth signalled the start and Locomotion No. 1 moved off. The engine at first struggled with the eighty-ton train and its 553 passengers, but gradually the little engine increased its speed to 8mph, accompanying coaches struggled to keep up.

Suddenly there were shouts from the wagon that carried the surveyors that something was wrong, as the wagon was jolting and jerking. The train was stopped, and it was found that the wagon was off the rails, but the power of Locomotion was such that it even pulled in this condition; the wagon was quickly hauled back on and the train continued, but the same thing happened again. This time it was found that the wheel was faulty and it was shunted into a siding, striking a bystander from Aycliffe, John Davison, who was badly shaken but not injured.

The train again continued, but on reaching Simpasture, Newton Aycliffe, it again ground to a halt, George Stephenson shouted that it was just "oakum in the feed pipe" and they worked thirty-five minutes and removed old rope from the pipe. Timothy Hackworth shouted "every man to take his own convoy", soon the work was finished and little Locomotion again chugged forward passing the level crossing at Aycliffe now (Heighington Station), and this is where the throttle was opened up and the speed was increased to 15mph.

At midday, the train arrived at Darlington; it had taken precisely two hours to cover nine miles, having three stopping's, its average speed being 8mph. The journey had been a resounding success. The Stockton-Darlington line showed what it was possible to attain, with Steam Locomotives, and it paved the way for an even larger project, that of the Liverpool-Manchester Railway and George Stephenson was appointed Chief Engineer, using his own Locomotive, Rocket, which vindicated this type of Transport and his fame spread. Stephenson asked the Pease family to acquire parliamentary permission for the use of Locomotives on the S&D Railway. It was actually Stephenson's 'Locomotion' that hauled the first train to Stockton on the 27th September, 1825 pulling 600 passengers in a total of 38 wagons a total of 21 miles from Shildon, at 15 miles an hour. After a year, the price of coal in Stockton halved because of the cheap haulage.

As stated earlier the S&D made its maiden journey on Tuesday 27th. September 1825; it commenced from the '*Masons Arms*', Shildon, the Pub had been quickly established in the town infact all future Railway operations began at this point. Heading on to Simpasture then Heighington Lane, by-passing the now '*Locomotion Inn'*, which later was an S&D Station then on to Darlington and Stockton. On the day there were a variety of disruptions mainly because of axel failures and the engine also developed a fault, this delayed the overall time by 55 minutes.

There was no dramatic effect on Shildon as by 1831 the increase in population totalled only 867; by this time there were two Inns the '*Grey Horse'* and the '*Masons Arms'*. A private contractor to the S&D Railway Mr. Daniel Adamson who also owned the *Grey Horse Inn* used a horse drawn coach '*Perseverance'*, to convey passengers to Aycliffe, Darlington and Stockton. In a very short period Adamson's coach was completing twelve journeys a week carrying an average of six passengers a journey.

Adamson built a Coach House opposite the *Grey Horse* and this became the first purpose built Railway Office. By 1833 the only room at the '*Masons Arms*', was taken over by the Railway Company and used as a booking office, there was also a Directors office and board room, a waiting room was also built at the other side of the railway. The railway & Station at the '*Grey Horse'*, was converted to a goods station. A further Inn was established at this time which was '*The Globe*', and this was used by the local society headed by Timothy Hackworth, its aims being to further the moral, intellectual needs of the local population in the face of increasing consumption of alcohol. Yet another Inn appeared and this was the 'Black Bull', and in a short time there was reported to be amazingly 400 pubs in the Shildon area.

By 1841 there had been a big rise in the Population of the area to 2631. Earlier in 1833 foundations for a Church was laid and within a year the Church was completed. Shildon was quickly getting noticed and in 1825 the Shildon Engine Works was built employing twenty people up to 1827; as Hackworth built '*Royal George'*, the workers doubled to 50. Hackworth decided to build his own works at Shildon taking Joseph Pease's advice and calling it 'Soho', in 1832. Eight years later he resigned from the post of Chief Engineer for the S&D railway, he had taken on this appointment when George

Stephenson moved to the post of Chief Engineer of the Liverpool

Modern day 'Grey Horse Inn', previously 'The Surtees: Owned by Daniel Adamson

Adamson's Coach House, across from the 'Grey Horse', The arch probably housing the coach can be seen around the small window on the left: Daniel Adamson senior

Manchester Railway. Hackworth concentrated on building his own business at his Soho works he designed and produced an engine for Russia built to very high engineering standards.

Shildon

In 1988 Shildon had a population of 14.000 in sharp contrast to 1800 when there was reported to be 100 people as part of a small Hamlet. The '*Grey Horse'* was the sole Inn and Daniel Adamson owned this. The community survived mainly on primitive coal mining, others were employed in agriculture and weaving (cotton). Local coal and also large quantities from other areas were brought through the village on packhorses to avoid tolls. The transportation of the coal cost 2/6 for each mile (12.5). The cost of this caused Industrialists and Colliery owners much concern. On Tyneside metal tramways using horse drawn trucks had been developed but the journey to port at Stockton made nonsense of this method; the experts also knew that if a new Railway haulage system was introduced, it would reduce the price of coal by 80%. The Pearce and Dixon families had completed a survey on using a canal for transportation of coal but it was later ruled out because of unsuitable terrain so by the time of the launch of the S&D Railway coal owners looked anxiously on, hoping for success.

The word spread quickly throughout the area and soon Mechanics and Engineers moved into the area of Shildon with their families. Streets of houses appeared like magic and soon street names like 'Railway Terrace', 'Station Street', 'Mechanic Street', came into being surrounding the Railway Works and this part of Shildon was called 'New Shildon'. By 1839 work began on an alternative route to Darlington and a tunnel was completed and opened on 10th. April 1842. The cost was an amazing £100.000 using 7 million bricks from the local brick works; this brickworks was established mainly to supply the demand for new housing and the new tunnel. The local Quarry also supplied stone for the tunnel and also some housing.

Eventually the opening took place and a new Station was built, making the one at the '*Masons Arms*', redundant and it became a reading room and a badly needed Library and Mr. Hamilton was appointed as Caretaker with a yearly salary of £825. The new station at Shildon became the last and existing station. The expansion continued at New Shildon when in 1841 a gas works opened to supply the Railway Company and also the Soho works. During the period of 75 years to 1900 no less than 29 pits were developed one of these being 'Dabble Duck', earning its name because the working conditions were so wet. This is now an Industrial Estate. Old Shildon by 1857 was further developed with a police Station then a much needed Post Office. The Quarry still existed and now there was an iron and brass foundry this was owned by Mr. Downing and it complemented Engineering in the area. Other tradesmen also prospered one being a Tailor who supplied the uniforms for the Railway Company staff. By this time it was noted there were 8 Public Houses of the eventual 400.

It was interesting the effect the S&D Railway had on Shildon and the Country in general if not the world as events were also closely scrutinised by America who later bought locomotives from the Stephenson's. It was also noted that at the Stockton and Yarm coal yards prior to the S&D, haulage was 18/- a ton and this was reduced to 12/- a ton then later to 8/6. This lower price attracted far more people to the fuel and with it high demand and expansion in the Collieries. By 1830 output was 16 million tons, by 1850 this figure trebled to 49.000.000 and by 1880 this was improved even further to 147.000.000. As time progressed the demand for coal got even better as high deposits of iron ore were discovered in the Cleveland Hills. This demand was created by the high amount of rail track and engine plate needed to satisfy the railways that were springing up all over the Country and on a visit to Middlesbrough Gladstone made his famous remark.

Steel output was 49.000 tons in 1850 but by 1860 Bessemer converter and other processors allowed output to increase to 1.440.000 tons by 1880. The Railways accelerated the growth of the coal, iron and steel industries. There was a tremendous demand for the rapid transformation of Southern areas and also for export; the massive profits from which accumulated new investment in the Railways and with it the coal industry. Between 1830 and 1850 approx. 6000 miles of Railways were opened in Great Britain, entirely due to accumulated profits leading to new investments in Rail Companies during the years stated. The establishment of the Railway and with it high production of coal gave England a big lead against all other Countries early in the nineteenth century.

The S&D layout at Shildon:

From Soho house the S&D continued westwards along Soho street to the Masons Arms and the Byerley Road, Madison Street Adelaide Street to the level crossing and it was here that Locomotion was first coupled to its train on the 27th.September 1825. The Inns did a roaring trade en-route. Very near to this point was the 'Railway Institute'; beyond the level crossing 'Shildon Wagon Works' was situated. The construction of an engine shed in Shildon was one of the objects of the Peases and indeed proposed. In the following years improvements were made 1848, 1852, 1854, 1856 & 1864. In 1886-1892 considerable work was completed and a new Turntable was evident in 1906. In 1915 one of the Workshops was specially fitted out to cater for Electric Locomotives. The running shed was closed in 1935 and the work transferred to a wagon repair shop.

Later in 1973 a large investment of £280.000 was forthcoming. Shildon was the largest wagon works owned by British Rail and covered an area of 43 acres, twelve acres of this is enclosed. The shops employed 2.400 people turning over £14.000.000; this was in addition to completing normal running repairs. This was found to be essential because various minerals carried especially from the giant ICI Company corroded the insides of wagons when the wheels and under frame was perfect. This kept new investment in new rolling stock to a minimum. The Company also took on work for other unusual wagons and designed the same. Output figures for the Company were new wagons 600-1000 and over 30.000 repairs and finally 2.400 re-body work; these figures show a considerable enterprise and the expertise, of speciality tradesmen saving the Country and B/R. millions because mainly of renewing the life of rolling stock.

From the Masons Arms, the S&D continued northwards along Byerley Road towards Bishop Auckland; about 1000 yards further up the hill is crossroads, the main road turns right. On the left was the '*Surtees Arms'*, later '*The Grey Horse*' before reaching the cross roads, on the right hand corner is Daniel Adamson's coach house, with arches on all sides that have been filled in with stone. This is a valuable relic of the S&D Railway. From Soho works a private Company built a series of lines to service their family owned Royalties, this was the historical Surtees family and the Railway was known by that name. When using S&D lines the accepted dues were forthcoming.

Facing eastwards along Main Street the track takes a gentle turn to the right beyond the Coach House, the Masonic Hall is seen at the junction of Middleton, Alma and St. John's Road. Soho can be reached by Hackworth Close, where Shildon Station is very accessible. From the Masons Arms the S&D could be again followed left to Brusselton inclines, by taking a sharp left signposted Thickley and Royal Oak the other road continues to West Auckland. The Brusselton road is the boundary of Shildon Wagon works; this joins the original track to the summit and the host of Collieries that were the reason for the S&D in the first place.

In 1947 when the National Coal Board took over they took over 8 mines in this small area and there was a similar amount still in private hands. The Collieries employed 2000 men with an annual turnover of 500.000 tons of coal. At the summit of Brusselton at the east incline the wagons were lowered by rope to be coupled to Locomotives at the Masons Arms. The winding engine was just an ordinary 60 hp powered and the same engine handled the full wagons at the western incline.

In comparison with other inclines in Durham these were a modest 1 in 30 range, while at Ingleby on the Rosedale branch it was I in 5 in places. At Brusselton 2 rows of buildings including houses were demolished. With the general decline of mining in the area it caused a kick back in Shildon Yards and West Auckland sheds closed. It also cost thousands of jobs and new industry had to be

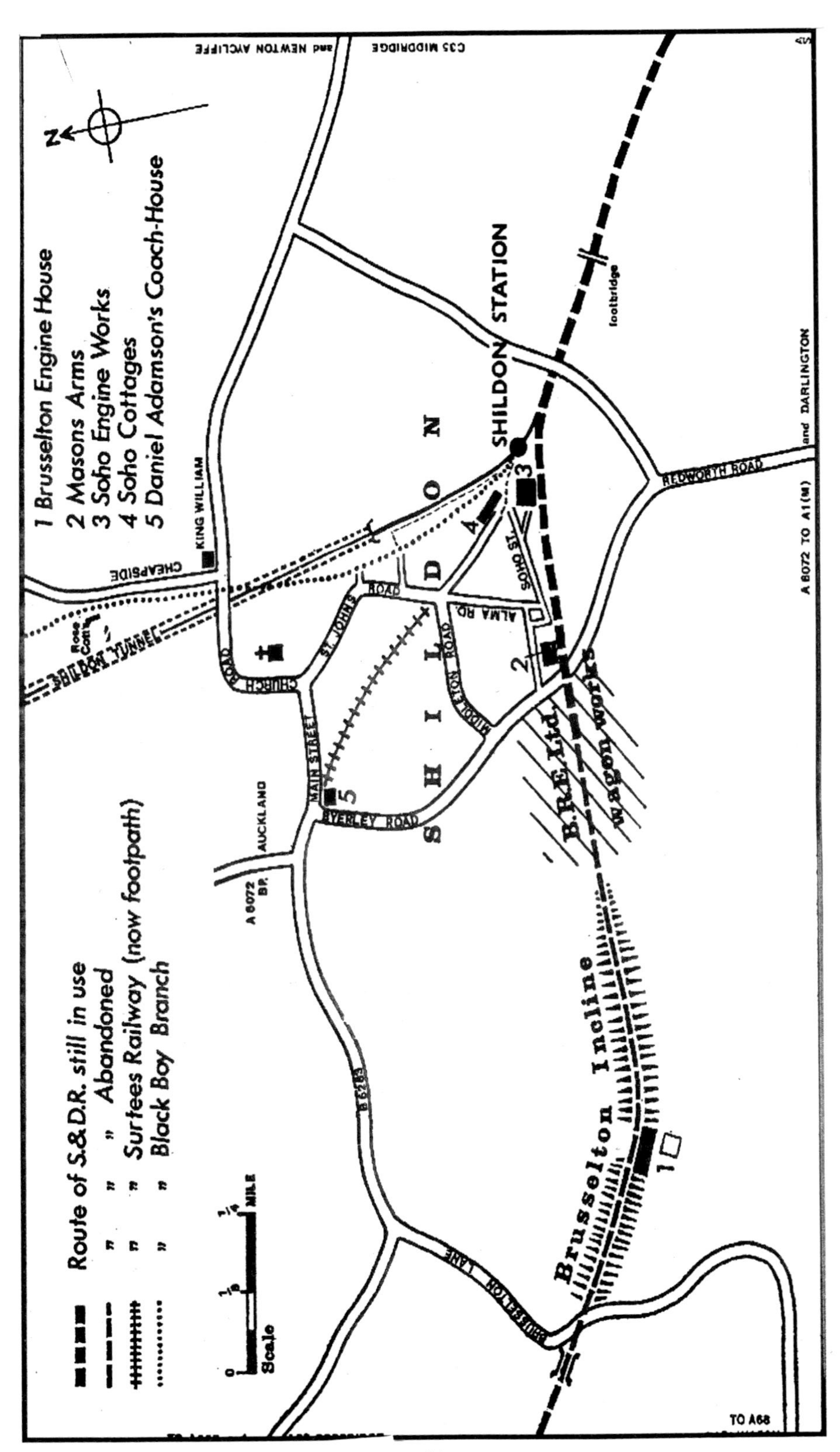

1 Brusselton Engine House
2 Masons Arms
3 Soho Engine Works
4 Soho Cottages
5 Daniel Adamson's Coach-House
Route of S.&D.R. still in use
" " " Abandoned
" " " Surtees Railway (now footpath)
" " " Black Boy Branch
Scale
MILE
N
SHILDON STATION
SHILDON
footbridge
B.R.E. Ltd.
Wagon works
Brusselton Incline
BRUSSELTON LANE
REDWORTH ROAD
A 6072 TO A1(M) and DARLINGTON
TO A68
B 6283
AUCKLAND
A 6072 BP.
BYERLEY ROAD
MAIN STREET
CHURCH ROAD
ST. JOHNS ROAD
MIDDLETON ROAD
ALMA RD.
SOHO ST.
CHEAPSIDE
KING WILLIAM
SHILDON TUNNEL
C35 MIDDRIDGE
and NEWTON AYCLIFFE

The New 'King William Hotel',

introduced to southwest Durham quickly. Jobs eventually came to

The top of the 'Black Boy Incline',

the area, not as many, but they were easier, cleaner and were of a better standard than living dangerously with grime and dirt of the industrial revolution.

Black Boy

The Railway progressed to the 'King William', Inn on the corner of the north side of Church Street, Shildon is very near to this point, and the Black Boy engine house with its stationary engine was situated here. This operated the inclines on both sides; the inclines drop away from Rose cottage and is now used as a short cut between Coundon Grange and High Shildon. Going a further 500 yards towards Eldon Bank Top there are amazing panoramic views over North & West Durham, until lowering the eyes to the dust and grime filled Colliery cottages. There is another incline on the Northern side of the ridge and continues in the area where Crossleys Eldon Brick works was situated. A further line ran parallel to the main road at Eldon. The high embankment of the present line to Bishop Auckland was evident with the tower of South Church beyond it. At Eldon Bank Top it is about a mile from Shildon Station which would complete the Shildon S&D system.

The Towns and Early Layout of the S&D Railway

The S&D Railway was initially planned for the Peases to transport their coal from their Collieries at Witton and areas to coal markets. It also had a huge affect on other areas en-route especially as the years progressed. The Western Terminus was at the 'Phoenix Pit', at Witton Park. Darlington however was a larger community than Witton and it was also where the bulk of the investment for the Railway came from. With this in mind the Peases and other Directors made sure Darlington was developed first. The S&D main line therefore was sighted west of Shildon initially across two ridges later these were by-passed by a route taking in Shildon and Bishop Auckland, even in the present day this represents the passenger service from Darlington to Bishop Auckland.

North of Shildon there is an east west ridge rising to a 500-foot contour that was a considerable obstacle to the original S&D Railway. The line crossed it on the slant by the two Brusselton inclines. The Black Boy branch crossed the ridge from Shildon in a northerly direction by another pair of inclines and it was built to service the Collieries on the north side. In April 1842 the Shildon Tunnel opened; three Directors, Joseph Pease, Thomas Maynell and Henry Stobart constructed this without Parliament permission.

This was a complete success in the haulage of coal wagons, without having to negotiate inclines; but also now passengers could be carried. Branch lines were built to South Church and also as far as Crook and Bishop Auckland. The Peases also arranged for a horse drawn Carriage Bus to connect with the southern rail head of the 'Durham Junction Railway', at Rainton Meadows, some 5 miles north east of the centre of Durham City. By November 1843, the line was extended from South Church to Crook, via Bishop Auckland. The line even went as far as the Phoenix Pit at Etherley.

This route by-passed the original Etherley inclines and the S&D Locomotives took advantage of this to haul via. Bishop Auckland. After the Shildon Tunnel was erected there was now single line track inside the tunnel to provide clearance mainly for present day stock. When emerging from the other side the track again doubles as it swings around the limestone ridge towards West Auckland and on to the high embankment with Coundon Grange on the right of Dene Brook. Here there was clear evidence of years of concentrated mining; the seam in this area was rich in quality coal. The North bank was owned by the Bishop of Durham and leased to Bolckow and Vaughan, the famous Iron Masters. The 'Durham Coal Company', exploited the other half of the Royalty owned by the 'Earl of

Eldon'; the area was so good that both parties worked very close to the boundary line.

The S&D Railway happily transported anyone's coal designing & laying track according to the area. The line originally came over the ridge as stated near the Black Boy inclines. At Eldon Lane at the foot of the embankment are the remains of the old limekilns built by Emmerson Murchamp, operating from December 25th. (Christmas Day) 1845. To the east of the kilns were railway houses; further north it crosses the South Church Spennymoor road. On the left side just before the bridge is a small rectangular paved area. This is thought to be the terminal point for S&D passengers taking the horse coach to Rainton Meadows.

Brusselton By—Pass tunnel and below the Brusselton Incline engine house at the time of a broken haulage rope:

The Brusselton Inclines were totally different and were the only connection with West Auckland and with the Haggerleases Branch running Westwards up the Gaunless Valley which was 4 miles long and was authorised by an act in 1824; but because of early financial difficulties by the S&D Railway not completed until October 1830. From this point the line serviced many Collieries always using the Brusselton Inclines. There was also a passenger service until 1858, and then it was diverted to the Shildon Tunnel Branch that ran from the North End of Shildon to West Auckland.

In 1853 the line from Barnard Castle was opened to Bishop

A birds eye photograph of the 'Etherley Incline' coal haulage system, the Engine house is in the bottom right corner.

Auckland making use of a mile of the Haggerleases branch line eastwards from Spring Gardens and also a mile of the tunnel branch of Fielden Bridge with the now direct rail connections, passenger trains could now avoid Brusselton Tunnel Branch. West Auckland became very important in the Railway system of the area; one of the most important North Eastern engine sheds was opened in 1887. Later in the century it had 46 engines based there and just prior to this there were 27 daily-booked mineral and passenger trains arranged from here. South of West Auckland Station the S&D crossed the river Gaunless using a very unusual Iron Bridge. In 1901 this bridge was dismantled and preserved at York Railway Museum.

Years later a new modern steel bridge was built exactly in its place to service the now very busy Brusselton Colliery. Taking the right fork road just through the village square to High Etherley, after crossing the river a house can be seen on the right, this was on a level crossing with the Haggerleases Branch. West of the crossing was a skew bridge which carried the S&D over the Gaunless at this point. Very near to here the Haggerleases branch climbed towards Evenwood Station crossing a viaduct then turning northwest to the Butterknowle branch terminus.

Later when the Barnard Castle line closed the line still serviced Randolph Colliery. Later when Randolph closed so did this railway. Getting back to the Etherley level crossing proceeding to the top of High Etherley the road proceeded left to Tow Law; going through Etherley Village about a mile towards Low Etherley and Bishop Auckland. The route of the S&D railway is evident here this was also the Etherley North Incline. The Line went through an under bridge, just before the bungalow which was on the left this section of the line and the Phoenix Pit closed early after the opening of the 'Wear Valley', line.

Shortly after the Etherley inclines closed, the winding engine was offered for sale. The bridge and old workings were filled with rubble. The Bungalow became the '*Railway Bridge Inn*', continuing into the present century, though the line closed about 1848. The site of the old Etherley engine house and the boarded engine mans cottage could be seen close by. The S&D continued northwards from Low Etherley towards a very high embankment and at the foot of it was a small stream. This leads to Phoenix Row and continues northwards.

Bishop Auckland

The layout at Bishop Auckland is very unusual, the station being triangular. Straight ahead there is a line to Crook that served Weardale branch having a very important cement factory on route at Eastgate. There is only one platform on this route and trains going in an opposite direction used a loop. Actually Bishop Auckland could only be reached from the east and the line that originally serviced Willington, Durham and Brancepeth came away to the right with the east signal box in the corner of the platform.

Middlesbrough Extension

As coal production increased it became increasingly evident that Stockton was unable to cope with the larger vessels now required. The S&D directors therefore met on 19th. October 1827 to explore the options open to them. The Yarm, Stockton members voted for another cut in the Tees at Portrack and extend the Stockton Staithes, but the Darlington Directors won the vote to extend the line further down the river. The Middlesbrough branch bill received Royal accent on 23 May 1828 and this provoked the first split in the board of Directors with resignations from Thomas Maynell (Chairman), and Leonard Raisbeck, assistant solicitor with Francis Mewburn.

The new Directors purchased 32 acres of land for Port Darlington, *(the Stockton Directors not liking this name at all)* The Directors further proposed to build a new Town 'Middlesbrough', and the very first town to owe its existence to the S&D was born. The site for the new Staithes was here at Port Middlesbrough but first the Tees at Stockton had to be bridged; proposals were put to the Tees Navigation Authority and were rejected. Finally plans were submitted for a Suspension Bridge (*First in the World*) that was designed by Captain Samuel Brown, RN. And these were approved. The Bridge was built in 1830 and it extended from Peel Nook, Stockton, in the present day this is (Bowesfield Junction) to Carr Housefield, Thornaby, a distance of 400, feet and 16 feet wide and twenty feet above water at Spring tide.

As time progressed it was found to be inadequate for heavy loads and by 1844 it was replaced by a girder bridge designed by Robert Stephenson. The bridge had masonry piers and when the present bridge was built in 1907 these piers were retained. The S&D erected 6 Staithes to load the incoming coal at Port Darlington and these were retained after being offered out to the public for a prize of £150 for the best idea and design and won by no other than Timothy Hackworth.

Stockton & Hartlepool Railway.

This Railway was started in May 1839 without Parliament permission and actually was an extension of the Clarence Railway and ran to Hartlepool. The Company built a station in Norton Road, Stockton, this was near the Clarence Station and it used all of the Clarence facilities as far as Billingham. From here they ran a further 8 miles to Hartlepool, by passing Cowpen Bewley, Greatham and Seaton Carew. The mineral line was opened in November 1840 and then it opened for passengers 9 February 1841. Eventually the Stockton and Hartlepool Railway and the West Hartlepool Harbour and Railway Company amalgamated on 1st. July 1851:

Darlington

The original route of the S&D Railway from the north was the arrival point at Bank Top Station; at the Station there is still a plaque saying 'Stockton & Darlington Railway 1825'. This area of Darlington grew with the S&D Railway and was very industrialised when all of the raw material and manufactured products were dispatched from the Station. Later in 1902 Robert Stephenson and Hawthorne Limited took advantage of this facility when moving their vast manufacturing business from Newcastle. This Company turned out one Locomotive after another and this was another classic example on the control the Stephenson's had over the Countries Rail system at that time.

Robert Stephenson knew that Brunel's gauge on his railways in the South West which included the '*Great Western*', would all eventually be obsolete and Brunel's smooth and steady running rail trains of 7.25 feet would have to conform to the rest of the Country and the Stephenson's gauge of 4.8 ½. Around 1878 all of Brunel's lines and Stations actually were converted to the Stephenson's gauge.

Darlington Bank Top Station is actually not situated on the East coast main line and this allowed non-stop trains to pass directly through the Station. This installation dates from 1st. July 1887, and features an amazing triple arched roof, each span being 60 feet and 1000 feet long. There was a single large island platform with a row of buildings along the centre. Outer platforms contain platform 1 & 4. North expresses used platform 1 on the east side; because of a clever new signalling system and rack layout, down trains can use either number 4 or number 1 platforms; 2 & 3 are the bays at the south end. Initially there were two additional roads between these platforms, so that traffic on the Saltburn, Richmond branches could run round their trains. At the north end of the Station the approach road comes up between platforms 1 & 4, so there is no direct contact between the extreme ends of the Platforms. On the east side of the approach there is a loading dock, while on the other there are two platforms 5 & 6, which are now used for the service to Bishop Auckland, but years ago this was used for Tebay and Penrith as well.

The main Historic features left by 1975 at Bank Top were two preserved Locomotives, '*Locomotion*', and '*Derwant*'. *Derwant* operated on Pease private lines until 1898. The largest masonry bridges on the original S&D line was 'Banomi's Bridge', across the river Skerne, just east of the Great North Road. Banomi also was the architect who designed 'Durham Gaol'. Banomi's Bridge was immortalised by John Dobbin showing '*Locomotion'*, with its array of wagons and other rolling stock on its inaugural run. North Road was the area where 'North Road Shops', produced quality goods well into the nineteenth Century employing 3.500 men, said to be the best class tradesmen in the world. This included Platers, Welders, Fitters & Turners; infact any Engineering trade could be learned at the works apprentices received a good basic grounding in whatever they did. Just prior to the First World War, 1000 woman were employed as part of the 'Darlington National Projectile Factory', producing munitions.

Bank Top Station, opened July 1887; three shed roofs can be seen with a train leaving No1 platform heading south:

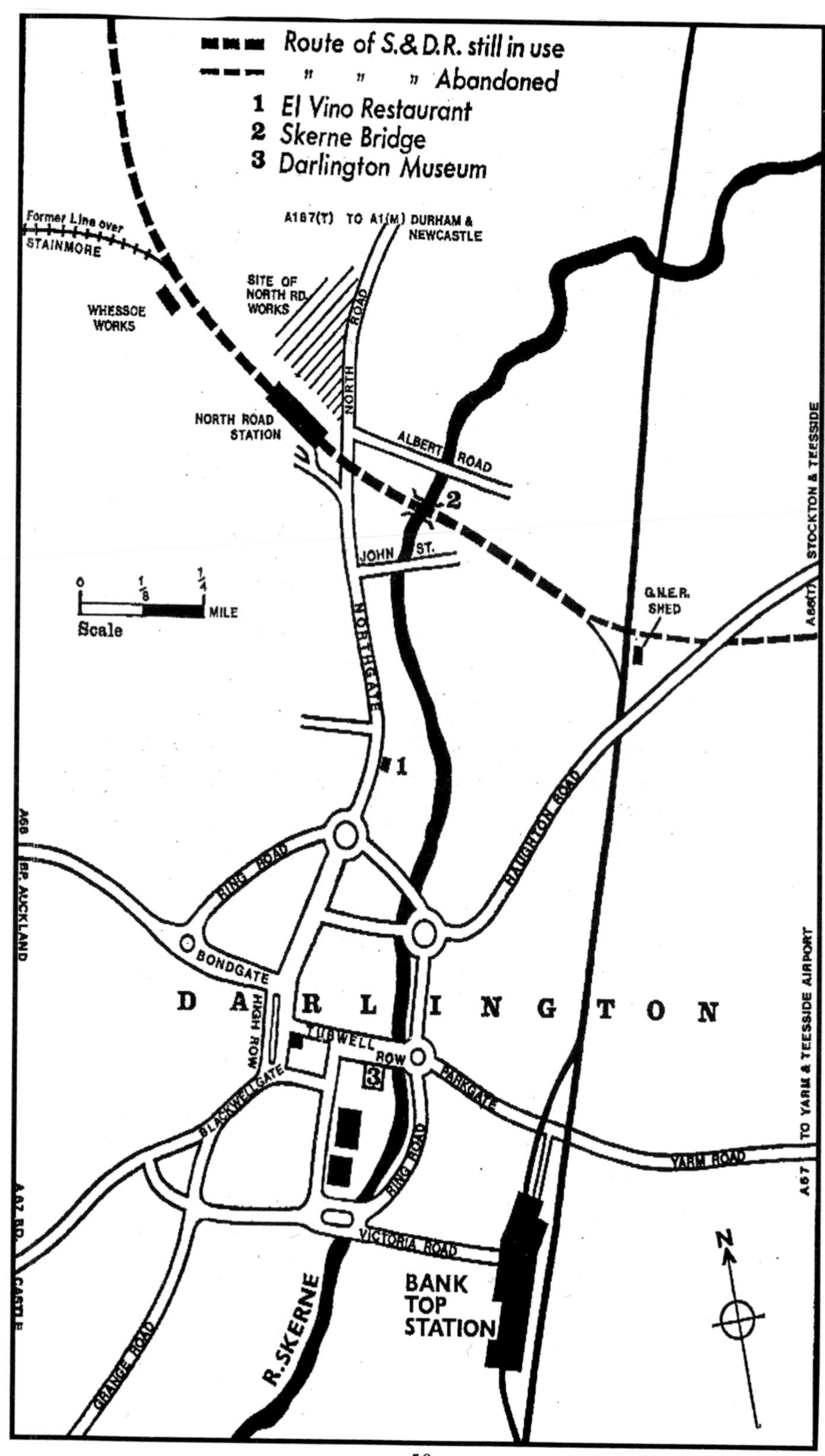
Route of S.&D.R. still in use
" " " Abandoned
1 El Vino Restaurant
2 Skerne Bridge
3 Darlington Museum
Former Line over STAINMORE
A167(T) TO A1(M) DURHAM & NEWCASTLE
SITE OF NORTH RD. WORKS
WHESSOE WORKS
NORTH ROAD
NORTH ROAD STATION
ALBERT ROAD
JOHN ST.
Scale
MILE
NORTHGATE
G.N.E.R. SHED
STOCKTON & TEESSIDE
A66(T)
HAUGHTON ROAD
RING ROAD
A68 BP. AUCKLAND
BONDGATE
D A R L I N G T O N
HIGH ROW
TUBWELL ROW
PARKGATE
BLACKWELLGATE
YARM ROAD
TO YARM & TEESSIDE AIRPORT
A67
VICTORIA ROAD
A67 RD. CASTLE
BANK TOP STATION
GRANGE ROAD
R. SKERNE
N

North Road Station is now being preserved, this Station was on the original route of the S&D railway and slightly to the west of the Great North Road; the present Station is not the original Station but was built in 1840 and is a fine example of Victorian Architecture; in later years B.R. used it for an unstaffed stop and over the years it gradually run down.

Darlington North Road Station For many years a Rail Museum, just prior to going to press has been the subject of a £1.7 M refit by Darlington Council & re-opens April 2008 as 'Head of Steam'; the Museum houses 'Locomotion No. 1' and much more

Opposite North Road Station, Hopetown goods depot was established, rail access was made through an archway; this was at the far side of Whessoe Lane near the old Locomotive Works. The well-known 'Whessoe Limited' is very close to this point; the Company was formed by W.A.Kitching and manufactured many of the well-known and original Locomotives such as *Derwent* and *Pilot.* Hopetown Junction lies just beyond Whessoe; this part of the S&D ran to Barnard Castle and Middleton in Teesdale, Kirby Stephenson, and Stainmore Summit. This was a very high pass the first of such peaks in the world that a passenger train negotiated. And the early trains did this without a problem.

The Establishment Period of the S&D Railway

Although the S&D Railway was laid out there was still much work to be done to turn it into the Railway it was planned. All of the Colliery owners in the areas of Shildon, Crook, and Willington and as far as Witton Park Collieries looked on with anticipation. Rails had to be laid taking into account sidings for shunting along the way. Coal Staithes at Stockton Wharf to cater for the extra production of coal had to be built. The cash layout was still tremendous for the Directors of the Company, even at this stage. Soon revenue did start to filter in.

Contractors were charged, from Brusselton to Darlington 6d. a ton, to Yarm 1/1 ½. a ton,

Most of this early coal was supplied by 'Old Etherley Colliery', along with other Collieries at West Auckland, Eldon, Blackboy & New Etherley the Peases were certainly doing exactly what they set out to do in that they were getting their coal to market

Robert Stephenson & Hawthorne Company came south to Darlington to satisfy the demand for quality Locomotives:

Stockton 1/3d. a ton. Overall there was an immediate reduction at coal markets at Stockton; this was from 18/- to 12/- a ton, there was a further reduction to 8/6d.a ton. This is exactly what all of the S&D supporters had hoped for. Yarm received their first coal from the S&D Railway on 11 October 1825, when the depot opened to the public on the 17th.and there was a celebration dinner at the '*New Inn Hotel'*, that evening to thank the gentlemen of Yarm involved.

teething problems were evident from a variety of things along the way, there was a shortage of wagons and from time to time there were Locomotive problems. For all of this in the first three *month 10.000 tons of coal was carried paying dues of £2000. Lansdale dues were charged by the Proprietors at 4d. a ton each mile, but for export this was reduced to ½.d a ton.*

The Earl of Durham, then Lord Lambton negotiated this export charge and it was called the 'Lambton Clause'. This was negotiated by him thinking that the S&D owners would not show profit; but they actually did show profit at this price. The Stockton Staithes were ready by January 1826 and the first steam coal ship was '*Adamant*', with a cargo of 168 tons mainly from 'Old Etherley Colliery'.

Passenger Transport

On the first of April 1826 S&D Railways gave Richard Pickersgill exclusive rights to run a passenger coach, when he leased the coach '*Experiment'*, for £200 a year. Alterations were made to it to carry twelve passengers on top for a fare of 9d. and about 150 passengers a day were carried. Also in April 'The Durham County Advertiser', announced that they would complete a daily service from Darlington at 8.30 am and 5.30 pm; from Stockton 8am and 4.30 pm. It was estimated that it would take 1 ½. Hours. At the same time Inn Keepers asked for a change in their licences to cover transport and Martha Howson of the '*Black Lion Inn*', in Stockton and Richard Scott of the '*Kings Head'*, Darlington placed two new coaches on the line, '*The Defence*', and '*The Defiance'*. On the 16th. October '*The Union*', Ran from the '*Black Lion*', & '*New Inn*', Stockton to the '*New Inn'*, at Yarm and '*The Black Swan'*, Parkgate Darlington. Within fifteen months seven coaches ran between Darlington and Stockton,

Experiment worked between Darlington and Brusselton until November 1827 when Dan Adamson of Shildon with '*Perseverance'*, as earlier noted, replaced this. Even with four passing places each mile it was difficult for coal handlers and passenger coach operators; regulations were laid down but it was hard to enforce, Locomotives had the right of way over horse drawn coaches and wagons. At inclines the descending train gave way; if they met in the middle the ascending engine reversed. Loaded wagons drawn by horses were given precedence against other coaches.

Croft

The Croft Branch which was east of the Skerne Bridge opened for traffic 27th.October 1829, this used the northern end of their main line York to Darlington it was situated directly on the coal depot at Croft:

Heighington Station,

This Station was situated either side of the road and had a covered roof and was rather long. Situated either side of the line was a 'Royal Ordinance', factory which employed hundreds of people; immortalised these days as the 'Aycliffe Angels', they were very brave ladies and some travelled from long distances to catch their local S&D Railway to the plant. From time to time because of handling high explosive, accidents and explosions happened but this did not deter these ladies who worked ceaselessly & bravely to keep our army supplied.

The S&D Railway played a major part in getting people to and from the factory especially during the war when petrol was scarce, the Rail Company of that day was operating thousands of special passenger trains each week for the Government factories. The long shelters could still be seen years after the war at the Heighington Station and they indicated just how many people waited for trains over that period. The London & North Eastern Railway Company who owned the railway at this time was requested to provide transport for up to 30.000 workers a day. The Company did this by using two sections, one of these was the 'Simpasture Branch', and a special station was constructed which was a 4 platform Station handling passengers from Bishop Auckland. Another Station also magically appeared and that was 'Demons Bridge', and this terminus handled people from Teesside, Hartlepool and Seaham areas, leaving Heighington to cover Darlington. The Complete set up actually carried 12.000 passengers each day in 20 trains that serviced the factory each day.

Two miles south of the station was a boggy section and initially rail could not be laid; George Stephenson was faced with massive problems and his navvies filled the area with stone and other material. For some reason the bog kept moving sideways and the following mornings it would seem that fairies or a phenomenon had interfered with their completed work from the day before. A local farmer did not make things any better when arriving every day to make sarcastic remarks; this was John Potts who lived at Dene Head, which was the first farm on the left westwards along Coatham Lane. Eventually Stephenson and his navvies conquered the bog and the rail was laid; this experience must have been handy for Stephenson as he was faced with similar but far greater problems later in his career with Chat Moss, this was on the Liverpool Manchester Railway, after he was appointed Chief Engineer and after many others had tried Stephenson finally succeeded.

Accidents

Later in the century it was inevitable as more trains were introduced to the line there would be accidents; most could have been avoided. Some miles south of Shildon on the morning of 16th. November 1949 there was a serious collision; a Freight Train had called at yards in the early hours and loaded with girders. The train set off for Darlington and the last 14 wagons and the brake van became detached from the rest of the train, neither guard was alert enough to realise what had happened even though the train had only travelled 1340 yards in 30 minutes since leaving Shildon.

Suddenly they heard the approach of the 5 am. Locomotive from Crook to Darlington; they both jumped off the van just in time before the train crashed into it. The impact was tremendous and the wagons ended in a heap and it demolished number 9 bridge south of Heighington. Fortunately no one was hurt or killed despite the fact that the passenger train was carrying 120 people in three coaches. Colonel D.McMullen in his official report on 30th. January 1950 blamed the Signalman at Heighington for not noticing the train was incomplete and also the Signalman at Whiley Hill for not correcting the situation, because having doubts about the completeness of the train he took no action.. This was a prime example how accidents could happen and also that they could be avoided by the diligence of Signalmen; their Locomotive was one of the Tank Engines running bunker first.

In October 1943 there was another accident involving a passenger train. Train driver Syd Midgley a fireman & G.Young were working the late train from Bishop Auckland one evening as they came under Drinkfield Bridge near Whessoe House, the Locomotive came off the rails and the coaches quickly followed. Surprisingly on the curve the wheels sank into the ballast and the Locomotive leaned over at 45 degrees towards the other line, but because of prompt action by the crew they prevented the train coming from the opposite direction from crashing into the wreckage.

The Clarence Railway Challenge

Near Simpasture the S&D line turns westwards to Shildon and at this point the Clarence Railway and its Chairman Christopher Tennant (*a life long enemy of the Peases*) had stolen a march on its rival the S&D. Some time before the S&D line appeared, the Clarence had built a line to the area mainly with the intention of servicing the Collieries. This line ran directly to the Tees and was shorter than the S&D route. This was 11.5 miles to Haverton Hill coal depot a further 5 miles from there to the coal drops at Stockton was 17.5 miles. The S&D route was 17.5 miles to their coal depot and 21.5 miles in total. The Clarence Bill received Royal Accent in May 1828 taking its title in honour from the Duke of Clarence (later William 1V) the main line ran from Samphire Beacon (Port Clarence), a junction was completed with the S&D at Simpasture to give access to the Collieries. One branch came from Norton Junction to Norton Road, Stockton; another proposed route to Durham actually ran to Thrislington. The Sherburn Branch to Coxhoe and a further branch to Byers Green. The first export coals came to Stockton Junction on 29th. October 1833, to Haverton Hill in January 1834 & on completion of the line to Port Clarence in 1834. A loading facility was established at Port Clarence. Obviously the cheapest route was the Clarence Line but the Pease's owning the major part of the facility undermined

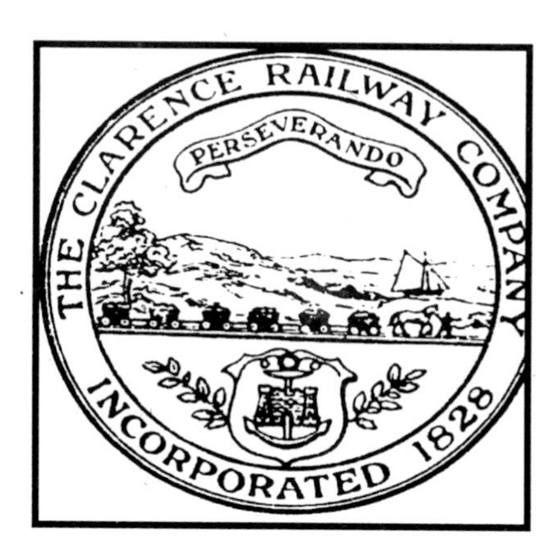

Clarence Railway Seal:

Tennant and his Company beyond belief; one of the ways they did this was by prohibiting all Clarence coal leaders from operating during the hours of darkness while their own leaders were allowed to do this. S&D wagons were only counted,

Christopher Tennant, from Stockton he moved to Hartlepool in 1832 where he formed the 'Clarence Railway Company', (1836-1842) mainly to service areas like Coxhoe, Spennymoor and Byers Green, the coal being shipped from Hartlepool, Tennant died in 1839 :

while the Clarence equivalent were stringently weighed carefully. They further undermined the Clarence by charging the Coal owners far more for haulage on the Clarence shorter route. The Clarence found themselves sadly in considerable difficulty because of this action; this was a classic example of the Pease power in these areas and the advantage the rich and poor divide that existed at that time.

The rivalry lasted between

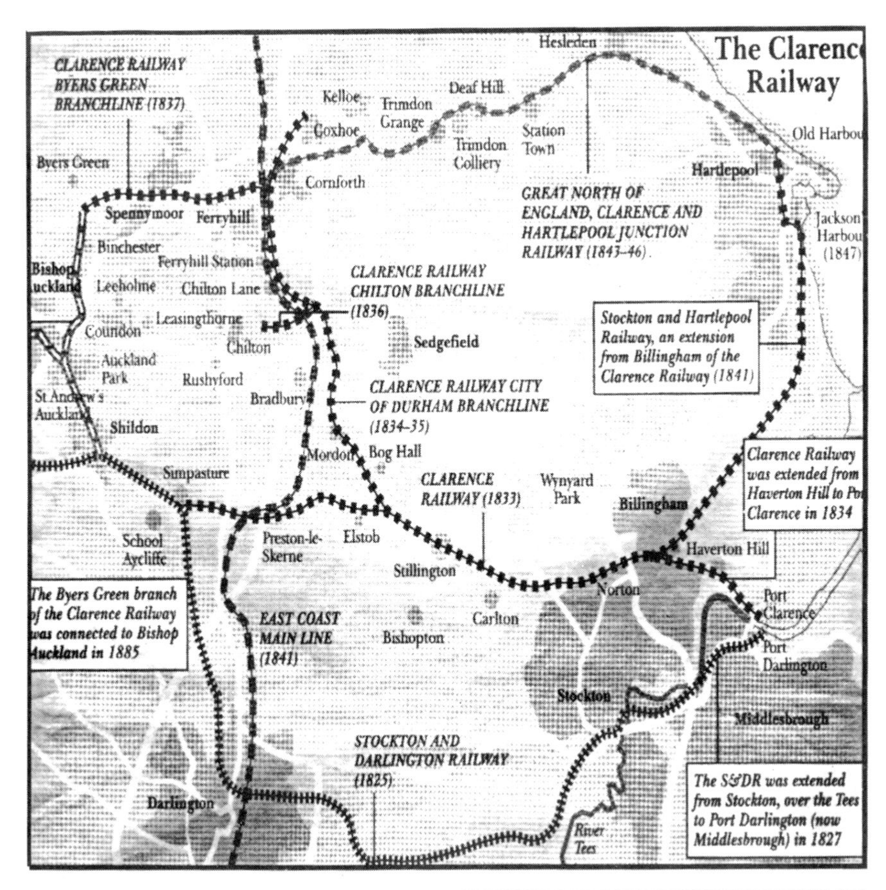

Above a layout of the Clarence Railway and also Ralph Ward Jackson who was a rich Solicitor from Eston who arranged the re-routing of the 'Clarence Railway', to his new Landing', at Hartlepool in June 1847.

After the death of Christopher Tennant the founder of the Railway. under the guidance of Ralph Ward Jackson the railway prospered; when leading coal from Coundon, Leasingthorne, Roddymoor, Bowburn, Crowtrees, North, South & East Hetton, Coxhoe, West Cornforth.

By 1852 the ownership of the Clarence passed to the control of 'Jackson, West Hartlepool and Dock Company', and by 1865 was taken over by the 'North Eastern Railway:

these two Companies as long as the two Companies were established. Rich Southern people also backed the Clarence fight but to no avail. The Clarence was taken over by the Hartlepool Harbour & Railway Company in 1853, and then finally it was taken over by the 'North Eastern'. Two years earlier this same Company had taken over the S&D Company. In later years this powerful new North-Eastern Railway Company took a look at both routes and not surprisingly the Clarence route was used for all coal traffic routes to the sea markets, while the S&D handled the Freight traffic. By 1913 coal production peaked at 287 million tons and the North Eastern Railway Company modernised this to Electricity.

John Dixon

Wherever George Stephenson was working, Dixon was not far away; he was credited as being second in line to Stephenson as the world's first civil engineer. John Dixon was born at Cockfield in 1796, the grandson of another great man, George Dixon, who was credited as promoter of the 1767 canal scheme.

This is also the year that his brother surveyed, 'The Mason Dixon line', between Maryland and Virginia from Pennsylvania in America. The Dixon family owned a colliery at Cockfield, Co. Durham, which was sold to Jonathan Backhouse in the same year that John was born; Backhouse, was related to the Dixon's through marriage.

As John Dixon began to work,

John Dixon of Cockfield born 1796, brilliant surveyor, the same family who surveyed the 'Mason & Dixon line' in America; worked for the S&D railway then later with George Stephenson.

Backhouse suggested he work for S&D as a clerk. When he was twenty-four, George Stephenson changed all this when he took him on, as his assistant. Both got on very well and in 1827 Dixon left S&D to work with Stephenson on the Liverpool and Manchester project. The experience gained, getting the line over Chat Moss, placed him amongst the best civil engineers in the world. Dixon finally returned to S&D railway in 1845, as a consulting engineer and this is when he had a direct conflict with John Harris who also was a Quaker engineer. John Dixon died on 10th October 1865, from bronchitis, at his 'Belle View', home on Coniscliffe Road, Darlington. In the present day the 'Ropner Group', of Companies were based at this large Quaker mansion.

The Liverpool & Manchester Rainhill Engine Trials The Company directors who arranged this were only interested in the best engines to work on their line and to this end organised the 'Rainhill Trials' in October, 1829, when stringent rules and conditions had to be observed. Each locomotive had to travel 37.5 miles twice, representing the return trip, each hauling the required load.

Belleview', which was John Dixon's home in Darlington, later was the headquarters of the Ropner Group of Companies. Dixon died in 1865:

Stephenson had entered the *Rocket,* which was far superior to his earlier Locomotion and came out the winner, winning the £500 prize after completing all of the tests required. In the celebrations for the opening day which was 15th September 1830; a very eminent guest also attended the trial Prime Minister of the day, the 'Duke of Wellington'.

Another man exhibited a locomotive at Rainhill that day, his name was Timothy Hackworth. Hackworth had a special relationship with the Pease family, especially Joseph; Hackworth eventually built the famous '*Sanspariel'* the engine that would just miss out in trials against the '*Rocket'* (Stephenson's) and other well-known engines of the times. But the disadvantages, against which Hackworth worked, are very well known.

The '*Sanspariel'* breakdown was said to be the fault of Robert Stephenson & Co., who cast and bored the cylinders, this was denied by them. The water pump was later found to be faulty. The end product, and design were, in many respects, far better than the '*Rocket'*. The original '*Sanspariel'* could be seen working on the Bolton Leigh Railway, after seven years not much the worse for wear, the boiler never ever requiring essential repair, when most of its rivals were on the scrap heap.

After the trials at Rainham, most leading engineers started building locomotives; they were

1829. GRAND COMPETITION of LOCOMOTIVES on the LIVERPOOL & MANCHESTER RAILWAY

STIPULATIONS & CONDITIONS on which the directions of the Liverpool and Manchester Railway offer a premium of £500 for the most improved locomotive engine.

I. The said Engine must 'effectually consume its own smoke', according to the provisions of the Railway Act. 7th Geo. IV.

II. The Engine, if it weighs Six Tons, must be capable of drawing after it, day by day, on a well-constructed Railway, on a level plane, a Train of Carriages of the gross weight of Twenty Tons, including the Tender and Water Tank, at the rate of Ten Miles per Hour, with a pressure of steam in the boiler not exceeding Fifty Pounds on the square inch.

III. There must be Two Safety Valves, one of which must be completely out of reach or control of the Engine-man, and neither of which must be fastened down while the Engine is working.

IV. The Engine and Boiler must be supported on Springs. and rest on Six Wheels; and the height from the ground to the top of the Chimney must not exceed Fifteen Feet.

V. The weight of the Machine, WITH ITS COMPLEMENT OF WATER in the Boiler, must, at most, not exceed Six Tons, and a Machine of less weight will be preferred if it draw AFTER it a PROPORTIONATE weight; and if the weight of the Engine, etc., do not exceed FIVE TONS, then the gross weight to be drawn need not exceed Fifteen Tons; and in that proportion for Machines of still smaller weight - provided that the Engine, etc., shall still be on six wheels, unless the weight (as above) be reduced to Four Tons and a Half, or under, in which case the Boiler, etc., may be placed on four wheels. And the Company shall be at liberty to put the Boiler, Fire Tube, Cylinders.

II. **There must be a Mercurial Gauge affixed to the Machine, with Index Rod, showing the Steam Pressure above 45 Pounds per square inch; and constructed to blow out a Pressure of 60 Pounds per inch.**

III. **The Engine to be delivered complete for trial, at the Liverpool end of the Railway, not later than the 1st of October next.**

IV. **The price of the Engine which may be accepted, not to exceed £550 delivered on the Railway; and any Engine *not* approved to be taken back by the owner.**

NB. - The Railway Company will provide the ENGINE TENDER with a supply of Water and Fuel for the experiment. The distance within the Rails is four feet eight inches and a half.

"Perseverance" "Rocket" "Novelty" "Sans Pareil"

exported to France and America. In America William Howard designed a Locomotive in 1828 for the Baltimore and Ohio Railroad. The locomotive Howard invented was never made, but Howard was credited with the patent. One that was built was '*Tom Thumb*' tested in 1829 and worked on the Baltimore and Ohio railroad in 1830. Designed by Peter Cooper of New York, it weighed about a ton with a single vertical cylinder of 3¼ inches diameter with a stroke of 14 inches. This engine decided the Americans to invest heavily in steam locomotives. Robert Stephenson & Co built a locomotive called '*America'* for the Delaware Company, which arrived in America about this time. It had outside sloping cylinders attached high on the boiler, one either side of the trailing end, with 4 coupled wheels.

Timothy Hackworth

Hackworth returned from the Rainham trials disappointed, but not disgruntled. The '*Sanspariel*' had displayed well and it had helped Timothy's reputation enormously. By the time he arrived back at his works at Shildon, he found an engine from Robert Stephenson, '*Rocket* No. 7'. It had 6 coupled wheels, with the cylinders fixed diagonally on either side of the boiler, between the middle and trailing wheels, after the type introduced by Robert Stephenson when he returned from America, in 1827. During the following two years, Hackworth decided to build, a more streamlined engine, faster and combining steadiness with reliability. Timothy named the engine '*Globe*' it had a copper cylinder steam dome to secure 'Dry' steam, 4 coupled wheels 5 feet in diameter, laminated steel springs, to all wheels, inside cylinders with crank axle, valve motion reversible by a single lever. The cylinders were 9 inches in diameter with a stroke of 16 inches, placed horizontally under the trailing end of the engine. The boiler was revolutionary, the steam generating and power was greatly superior to any other engines of the day, having the same area of heating surface.

Shildon & Hackworth

Hackworth's relationship with the S&D Railway was strange; by 1833 he resigned from their employment but carried on with a contract with them to supervise their Locomotives, together with the workshops and machinery. At the same time he carried on with his own business at Soho works where he completed Locomotives for Railway Companies including the S&D and countries as far away as Russia. The S&D actually developed this area of Shildon as early as 1825 with their own Locomotive works; when Hackworth resigned his post William Bouch was appointed as manager. The works were

Soho House where Hackworth planned his early work in Locomotives, the name 'Soho', suggested by Joseph Pease; today is a modern day Museum run by 'Sedgefield District Council' includes the families early way of life: below Mr & Mrs Timothy Hackworth:

independent and also carried out railway contracts in 1840 and these existed until the death of Bouch in 1876. When Hackworth died for some reason all of his machinery and facilities passed to the ownership of the Railways and closed in 1883, coming under direct control of Shildon Works. At this time these included S&D Railway all under the one umbrella of North Eastern Railways.

George Stephenson (Later)

When Forth Street Works was established mainly for the

production of mainly steam engines for the Railway systems, it was Edward Pease's confidence in Stephenson that got it off the ground, and Edward supplied the capital and so started a very successful business venture. Edward often referred to the Forth Street investments; he refused profit from war steamers supplied to the King of Sardinia on religious grounds.

***Sanspariel'*, built by Hackworth which just missed out in early trials against Stephenson's '*Rocket*':**

In 1821, George Stephenson was given the job by Edward Pease, of constructing the railways in the North of England and through it he would make his fortune. Stephenson can also lay claim to being the inventor of the safety lamp ironically named Davy's Safety Lamp.

The '*Rocket*', entered at the Rainham trials later seen at the Science Museum at Kensington showing cylinders now lowered:

It was said that Stephenson had been experimenting with this lamp while at Killingworth, even before Sir Humphrey Davy's discovery was made public in 1816. It was also said that he had made tests on a lamp a long time before Davy and that Stephenson was actually the inventor. In fact in January 1818 he was presented with a silver tankard from the public, together with a thousand pounds, for inventing the Safety Lamp. This presentation was indicated as testimony that he actually was the inventor of the lamp at least in the eyes of the locals.

John Harris

Another man from Darlington who also experimented, and indeed built, locomotives also at this time, was John Harris. In the present day there is a street named after him. He was credited with building the first '*Victoria'*, locomotive. Harris was also a Quaker and related through marriage to the Peases. Harris also completed contract work for the S&D Railway, when he carried out track repairs; this is the period when he fell out with the S&D accounts department. On the death of Timothy Hackworth Harris purchased the 'Soho', works and started to produce in-house locomotives, this upset many individual businesses, one being Kitching's Foundry at Hopetown who closed down.

Harris and Charles Lanson took over the Whessoe Bridge Building Company where some locomotives were produced, but he mainly concentrated on foundry work and engineering. He did, however, produce some locomotives namely '*The Derwant'*, '*The Victoria*', built 1863, the '*Kitching*', which was built at Hopetown, '*The Byron*', built 1868. The engines worked for 'The Consett Iron Company', and 'Londonderry's Railways', at Seaham docks they were strong machines and continued well until 1900. When the Darlington Stockton Railway, first opened it was certainly not sound. There was a lack of public confidence, resulting in Bankers withdrawing any further credit facilities Edward then later Joseph, took on the role of treasurer to guide the company through the hard periods. In a shareholder report on 9th September 1825 only 3 weeks prior to the official opening, doubts were raised whether it could pay its 5% dividend demanded by the main promoter. The project had mounting debts; even before coal drops and engine sheds had been constructed.

Further advancements had to be made; £40,000 from the Gurneys and £20,000 from Thomas Richardson, all guaranteed on promissory notes. This helped to meet the cost of the land purchase; at £25,000 but this exceeded the initial estimate by some £7000. There was also an amount of £32,000, which had been spent, on successfully opposing a rival Tees and Wear project in 1824. The scheme even owed Jonathan Backhouse, its Treasurer, £9342 for acquiring land on behalf of the company. Once again, Edward Pease came to the rescue of the Stockton Darlington Railway, when he agreed to meet the companies wage bill until new loans could be arranged; but gradually, the railway started to make money.

Woodside built between Coniscliffe Road and Blackwell Lane, owned by John Harris, below, one of John Harris's engine creations '*Derwant*'. Built at Hope-town; they were strong engines.

The Development of Mining In the North of England

In 1820 George Stephenson was engaged to lay a railroad connecting to Lord Londonderry's system to transport the Rainton coal to Seaham Harbour. Later in 1822 Stephenson was engaged to complete a further line to Sunderland after the 'Jane Shaft', was sunk at Eppleton. This particular line was opened on 18th. November 1822; the line was eight miles long. The railroad had three locomotives (*Puffing Billie's*), five self-acting inclined planes and five fixed engines. This was all part of a sophisticated transit system for the rapid movement of the coals to Coal Markets for home and abroad. Individuals began to come forward to push the coal industry forward one being John Robson; as Viewer for the Hetton Colliery Group, Robson took a leading part in the planning of this system and advised accordingly.

Roddymoor

As more and more Collieries were established around South Durham, other areas were considered; coal was the wealth of the times and promoters were eyeing West Durham, and the Crook areas as early as 1830 and certainly before the Durham 'County Coal Company' was formed. The Clarence Railway was considered at this time to haul the coal from areas around Roddymoor via. a branch line. The bill for this project was blocked in Parliament in 1836. Other problems were apparent mainly in connection with the lease; Capital was always the main problem and this eventually dried up.

Powerful men at the time saw the potential of the South West Durham coal production and formed another Mining Company the 'Northern Mining Company'. The group fully intended to build the Railway to the Collieries without Parliament permission. The Railway was called the 'West Durham Railway'. This enterprise ended slightly north of Billy Row; test sinkings went ahead in the area from 1836 and coal was found in abundance and was celebrated in 1841. It was at this time that John Buddle *(famous Viewer)* did a view of 'Roddymoor Colliery'; on checking the area at that time only farmers and sinkers were resident. The 'Northern Mining Company' ran out of funds by 1845 and the Peases bought the Company along with 'Jobs Hill Colliery'. The Pease family were heavily into coal mining at this time and they bought Collieries as fast as they were available to them:

William Coulson

Coulson was born at Gateshead Fell in 1791. He was undoubtedly one of the most eminent Colliery Sinkers in England. His sinking, up to the time of his death, was approx. a hundred & twenty pit shafts both in England and abroad, although a very high percentage of these were completed in the North of England. In 1862 he led a heroic band of sinkers, when they tried to get 400-trapped miners out of the pit shaft at Hartley Colliery

Thornley Colliery, Coulsons first

where they were entombed. An engine beam had broken in the shaft and trapped the miners deep in the bowels of the pit. Coulson was in the area when he heard about the calamity at the pit, and he had no hesitation in going straight there to try and get the men out. When he arrived everyone was at odds, and with his men he set to work with zeal and determination to clear the blockage in the shaft. Day after day they laboured, mostly without rest, and always the threat of gas and debris falling from above. Coulson and his men were not able to save any of the entombed men, but the sinkers never left their posts until all of the dead were out of that horrible pit. For their brave efforts William Coulson received a gold medal and his men were awarded silver medals from Queen Victoria. William Coulson was a self-made man, beginning his life not unlike George Stephenson *(famous engineer)* as a trapper boy at a Northern pit. Coulson was not educated, learning what he could on his own account. Having an inborn genius for surmounting the highest obstacles of nature. His energy and industry made his name as a brilliant mining engineer of the times, and he had amazing perseverance. Coulson had a family of four sons and three daughters. All of the family settled abroad, except for William, his son, who was with him at Hartley Colliery. He carried on sinking Collieries & was involved in a project putting a tunnel under the Mersey at Liverpool. He also founded an

Engineering Company at Crossgate Moor, Durham, where he lived.

William. Coulson (senior) in his early life, was employed at Walker Colliery, he worked a full shift at the pit, then travelled to the Tyne where he worked a further shift as a trimmer at the docks. He showed amazing energy and industry; especially in the Mining industry he came from a family of mainly Blacksmiths, his father grandfather and most of the Coulson descendants, worked for the Ravensworth Families for several generations. Coulson was involved in just about every Colliery sank in the North of England over the forty years up to 1865. Even with the pits he did not sink, Coulson was usually consulted. The worst type of obstacles were not a problem to him, with his practical knowledge and natural sagacity, problems melted away and he quickly progressed the sinking.

Hetton Colliery where Coulson found coal under the limestone band & where George Stephenson provided a Railway system:

His expertise and knowledge on sinking were even well known in countries abroad. For a number of years he developed mining resources in Prussia, mainly in the province of Westphalia. The work in these countries meant that he had to spend a great deal of time at sea, as well as on arduous trips in rough terrain overland. His gift for finding coal in the strata elevated him to high position amongst mining engineers of the day besides his engagements in Prussia, the Austrian Empire had the benefit of his great experience in developing mining resources in that country. He was also engaged in ironstone mining in Prussia. Two of the best-known collieries that William Coulson sank in Prussia were the Hibernia and the Banrock. He also sank a great many pits in Wales when he gave a service to the Newport and Cardiff Ironstone Company. It was not only solving problems abroad that William Coulson was famous, in this country there were many catastrophes which were linked to mining operations constantly happening when the North of England was trying to utilize its natural resources, and to keep people in employment. Mr. Coulson was the one who was always consulted. In December 1856, William Coulson was invited to a complimentary dinner, by a number of Durham and Northumberland dignitaries. The dinner was held at the house of John Gowland, in Durham City.

Local Sinkers & Mining Engineers in 1860 sank the shafts for Coal-mine Owners. They did an invaluable job for the industry; creating work for mining

Mr. George Johnson, who was an intimate friend of Coulson's, occupied the chair.

Through the chair he said he had known William Coulson for forty-five years. He was the first man ever to prove that coal existed below the magnesia limestone these were the Collieries of Hetton in 1821. He proved this point, much to the delight and happiness of all concerned, including landowners, government and ordinary miners who relied on the industry for their living. It was from that time that he began to rise in the estimation of mining engineers and colliery viewers and owners in fact *all* who were concerned in the development of Collieries.

Coulson went from one difficult sinking, to another, non-proved beyond his reach, and that included the east coast collieries of Seaham, and other coastal pits. Most of these were plagued by water, tide, and also sand. He had an uncanny knack of producing coal in the strata; it was as if he could detect it with a dousing rod. Just about all of the pits that he sank produced coal in abundance.

All that worked with William Coulson dedicated their lives to the North of England coalfield. All were aware of 'Strata Formations', and land layout. Many of the Coulson family can be seen together at Billy Row, on the 1851 Census with William Callerton, Harton, Hartley, Bedlington, North Seaton, Norwood, Crookhall, Roddymoor, Thickley, Pease's first Adelaide, Eldon, Blackboy (first pit), Whitworth, Bishop Middleham, Bowburn, Coxhoe, Crowtrees, West Hetton, Sherburn, Sherburn Hill, Philadelphia, Grange, Haswell, Thornley, Wingate, Castle Eden (two winning's), Seaton, Seaham, Framwelgate Moor, Waldridge Fell, Pelaw, and Urpeth. There were several sinking's in Lancashire, and

William Coulson and his men at Hartley Colliery where he failed to free the doomed miners:

Coulson, while sinking collieries like Roddymoor and others in the Crook and South-west Durham area. William Coulson and his associates were credited with somewhere in the region of 120 shafts up to 1865. Some of the best known are as follows: Whitley, Walker, Seghill, North Wales also five collieries in Prussia. West Sleekburn, Bewick Main, Peases Adelaide 1st & 2nd Collieries. Master Sinker William Coulson commenced his career as a sinker at Thornley Colliery, where he worked sixteen-hour shifts. He even obtained material needed to commence the contract the following day; this was on top of the sixteen hours worked. William Coulson was much respected by his family and his men, they were very confident in his judgment. So much so that they would unhesitatingly enter very dangerous places in connection with the sinking operations.

After Thornley the family concentrated on the Hetton Area putting in test borings with the intention of developing the area for the production of coal. For years it had been known that a thick band of Limestone Magnesia was evident right across the strata in the area and generally thought that no coal existed below it. William Coulson proved the theory wrong and bored into quality coal in abundance, below the Limestone, after which the Hetton Collieries were sunk; the Colliery was the first ever deep pit, it was 147 fathoms (1000 feet), deep and like all of the Coulson sinking's produced coal in abundance and was one of the most productive pits in Durham County; pleasing all parties especially land owners and ordinary people in the area, when the population doubled very quickly.

This opened the door to the Hetton Colliery Railways in 1821, and George Stephenson used Hetton for most of his experiments with Locomotives; then in 1825 the S&D railways involvement at Auckland, which William Coulson also sunk. As the Coulson's sank collieries one after the other George Stephenson was never far away; after Thornley was sank Stephenson designed the new railway from Thornley with a branch to Cassop and Ludworth. As previouly stated

The Railway opened 23 November 1835 and the line was completed as far as Haswell, en-route was Shotten and Castle Eden. In his private life Coulson was a modest and a quite man, who cared about people, he showed these attributes when

The Hartley Medals awarded to the brave sinkers; Coulsons was gold the others silver; designed by Mr. Wyon of the mint

risking his life to get the unfortunate men out of Hartley Colliery, when even aged seventy one, at the time of the accident, he toiled relentlessly, with one thought in mind that was to get these men back to their loved ones. When this was not achievable, there was no one more upset than Coulson, after which he toiled relentlessly on to get the dead out so that their families could give them a Christian burial, even with the constant threat of gas and falling debris, he and his men worked on, they did not relax until all of the men were at the surface.

Queen Victoria cried on hearing of the disaster, and she asked for frequent reports on if Coulson had managed to get the men out. Later at the inquest William Coulson gave the evidence that led to legislation banning the one-shaft collieries in England, and also the type of steel used for the manufacture of Engine beams. Later at a presentation the sinkers were presented with silver medals, for their brave attempts to get the men out, Coulson's medal was gold. William Coulson married twice; his second wife was Mary Hopper, who had a daughter Elizabeth, and son George by her previous marriage. Both of these children were shown to be born at St. Helens, Auckland. William Coulson sank St. Helens Colliery. They were shown on the 1851 census with their mother and stepfather living at 114 North Moor Cottages, Billy Row, and Crook. Joseph Coulson [authors G G Grandfather] lived at 110, North Moor Cottages, at this time they were sinking Roddymoor Colliery and other Collieries in the area. Earlier when sinking shafts at Durham, Whitwell, Bowburn and Coxhoe, Coulson lived at Shincliffe where he married for the second time.

Untimely Death:

On Monday 12th June 1865 William Coulson left his residence at Western Hill, Durham City, in his usual state of health. On this day he was due to attend a Consultation at Hetton Hall, the residence of Nicholas Wood esq. They were due to have a Consultation with respect to a projected new winning at Harton Colliery, near South Shields. The meeting had been due to take place at the Coal Trade Office, in Newcastle on Saturday. After the absence of Mr. Collingwood, and L. Wood, this meeting had to be postponed until Monday at Mr. Wood's house. William Coulson arrived at the house on time and entered into consultation with Mr. Charles Alderson, from South Shields, together with Nicholas Wood, and Mr. Collingwood. The meeting progressed well until William Coulson felt ill with an attack of Apoplexy, with which he was in much pain. Mr. Edgar, (Surgeon) was called

Marsden Colliery Sinkers
In the north of England a very difficult sinking was at Marsdon. This pit was commenced in 1877, and took over 7 years to complete. The total water dealt with at the time was 11,612 gallons a minute, this was for both shafts. When the pumps couldn't clear the water anymore it was decided to copy the Kind Chaudron system of boring out the water under water, to do this the diameters of the shafts were reduced to 14 ft. and the sinking under this system proved a success, incidently this system was first tried about 1850. Kind & Chaudren were the first persons to replace iron rods with wooden rods. The successes of this system was due to the wood being buoyant in the water, this allowing boring to greater depths.

from Chester Le Street, and also Mr. S.Shiell, who came immediately.

Mrs. Coulson and other members of his family were sent for and they quickly arrived, just before noon. Shortly after noon Coulson had another attack, after which he was in much pain. From the commencement of the problem until the evening, William Coulson appeared to be in a great deal of physical pain, and the entire time unconscious. At 6.15 that evening William Coulson died leaving his family very distressed. His body was conveyed to Durham City arriving there at 1 am. Tuesday morning. The funeral of William Coulson was held on Friday morning June 16th 1865 and it was exceptionally well attended with Dignitaries, Mining Officials, Mining Engineers, Coal Owners, and many just ordinary citizens who knew and respected him. His remains were buried at St. Margaret's Church Yard, Durham.

John Robson

Originated from East Rainton. Robson became a Colliery Viewer early in his life; later his main activity was to make sure that the remaining 'Stock's Row Companies', did not fall into the Pease control. John Robson promoted interests in the Collieries. In 1847 he resided at Redworth House and as agent sold shares in the 'Coppycrooks Colliery', near Shildon. Later in 1849 he was known to have lived at Whitwell Grange when selling shares of Collieries at Whitwell Grange and Framwellgate Moor. The Coulson's taking advantage of Robson's ownership of the Collieries carried out his sinking needs producing for him coal in abundance. William Coulson sank the last named Colliery at this time 'Framwellgate Moor'. As usual it produced quality coal in abundance. John Robson is highlighted in the book of the History of 'Eppleton Colliery', 'The Pit on the Down's'. The Colliery was part of a complex of Collieries owned by the Hetton Coal Company. In his capacity of 'Viewer' at Hetton he was called to give evidence at the inquest of the explosion at the Colliery. The jury found that the deaths were caused by accident from a pocket of gas which was ignited. Previous to the ignition the Colliery was adequately ventilated. It was noted that candle's were used at this time for lighting.

The Collieries along the Route of the S&D Railway.

The following Charts show a variety of up to 68 Collieries or drifts that were sunk and sighted near to the route of the S&D Railway. The owners of the Railway considered these Collieries when the Railway was planned. By 1947 most of the Collieries had been worked out and disappeared as not being

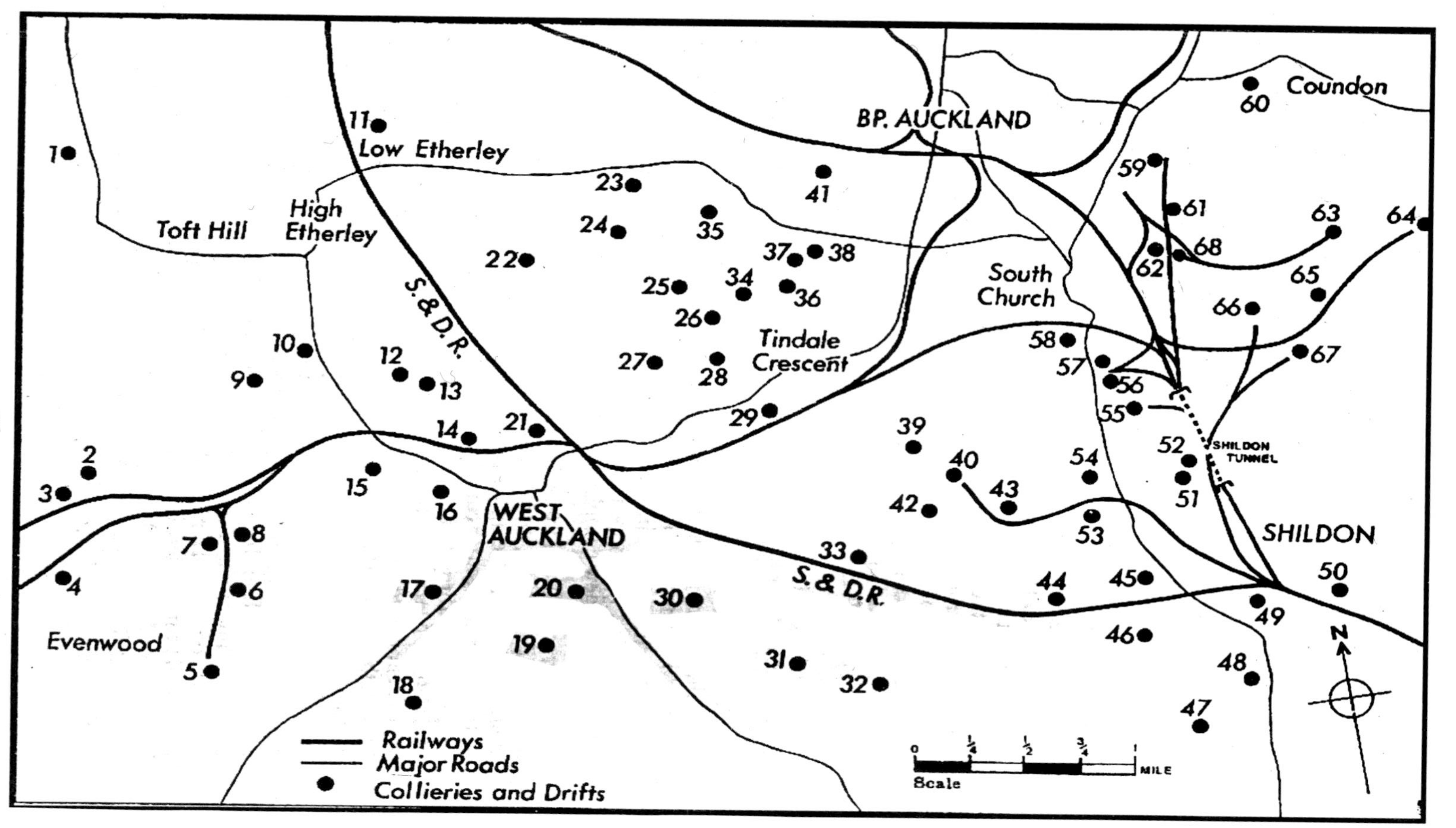
Coundon
BP. AUCKLAND
Low Etherley
High Etherley
Toft Hill
South Church
Tindale Crescent
S. & D.R.
S. & D.R.
SHILDON TUNNEL
SHILDON
WEST AUCKLAND
Evenwood
N
Railways
Major Roads
Collieries and Drifts
0 1/4 1/2 3/4 1 MILE
Scale

Key No. on Map	Colliery or Drift	Operating Dates
1	Carterthorne Colliery	1830s—1920s
2	West Tees (Railey Fell)	1863—1939
3	Gordon Gill (Little Gordon)	Unknown
4	Norwood	1830s—1904
5	Randolph	1893—1962
6	Tees Hetton	1830s—1894
7	Thrushwood	1821—1898
8	Evenwood Colliery	c.1840s—1896
9	Ramshaw Drifts	1936—1959
10	Gauger's Arms Drift	1940s—1960s
11	Old Etherley Colliery	1810s—1840s
12	Norlees Colliery—Crow Coal Pit	Pre 1860
13	Wood End Pit	c1940—c1963
14	West Auckland Drift	1930s—1967
15	Spring Gardens	1930s—1940s
16	West Auckland Colliery (Old Engine Pit)	1838—1925
17	Finlay's or Fiddler's Bank	1930s—1938
18	Staindrop Field House	1940s—1967
19	Hummerbeck	1880s—1897
20	Bildershaw	1930s—1957
21	West Auckland { Windlestone Pit / Steam Pit }	1838—1925
22	Etherley Colliery—Rush Pit	1911—1917
23	Etherley Dene Jumbo Pit (Probably Jam-Jar Pit)	1900s—1930s
24	Scales Drift	1930s (Only worked 2 years)
25	Woodhouses Colliery	1930s—1940s
26	St. Helens Colliery—"Brockenbacks"	1833—1926
27	St. Helens Colliery—Catherine Pit	
28	St. Helens Colliery—Emma Pit	
29	St. Helens Colliery—Engine Pit	
30	Ladysmith	1920s—1948
31	Brusselton Tower Drifts	1925—1963
32	Brusselton Colliery	1834—1968
33	Throstlegill Drift	1930s—1940s

Key No. on Map	Colliery or Drift	Operating Dates
34	Etherley Grange Colliery	1880s—1910s
35	Etherley Dene	c1900—c1910s
36	Woodhouse Lane New Colliery	1930s—1950s
37	Woodhouse Close Colliery Drifts	1930—1940s
38	Woodhouse Close Colliery	1837—1898
39	Haggs Lane	1950s—1964
40	Coppy Crooks Colliery	1835—1852
41	Etherley Lane Pit	1910s—1940s
42	Coppy Crooks (Spoor's)	1870s—1941
43	West Durham Wallsend Colliery	1890s—1906
44	New Shildon Drift	1949—1965
45	Furnace Pit	1866—1923
46	Thickley Colliery	1930—1953
47	Newhouse Drift	1935—1940s
48	South Shildon Colliery (All Saints)	1929—1958
49	Shildon Colliery ("Dabbleduck")	1866—1922
50	East Thickley Colliery ("Tennant's")	1829—1850s
51	Tunnel Drift	1936—1955
52	New Deanery Colliery	1945—1951
53	Shildon Lodge Colliery ("Datton")	1830—1924
54	Princes Street Colliery	1937—1958
55	Shildon Collieries	1820s—1830s
56	Deanery Colliery ("Brown's")	1810s—1840s
57	Adelaide's Colliery (Shildon Bank)	1830—1923
58	South Church Drift	1934—1940
59	Coundon Gate or Old Black Boy	1810—1830s
60	Coundon "Jawblades"	1920s—1930s
61	Black Boy (Later Old Black Boy)	1825—1860s
62	Auckland Park Colliery	1864—1943
63	Black Boy Colliery—Gurney Pit	1827—1928
64	Old Eldon Colliery—John Henry Pit	1864—1928
65	Eldon Colliery (South Durham)	1841—1930
66	South Durham (Later Old South Durham)	1830s—1860s
67	"Eldon Pits"	c1820s
68	Machine Pit—Old Black Boy	1825—1860s

These are a selection of original S&D Way Bills that were sent to me by Ken Robinson from Shropshire; they have never been seen prior to this; Ken worked in the S&D area at Witton Park as a Deputy for many years, and has a large collection of mining memorabilia. The bills were the weight of the Coal and Coke taken away from various Collieries in this area of Witton Park. They also record the destination of the Coal; some records the destination as being for the Iron Masters Bolckow & Vaughan.
The Phoenix Pit was actually know as Old Etherley situated at the bottom of the Etherley Incline and right on the western edge of the Railway.
Witton Park Colliery known as Etherley Jane Pit. There were many pits in the area at this time, another being called "Etherley George Pit", and were all situated on the south side of the River Gaunless.
Witton le Wear Colliery was also known as Marshal Hall Green Pit. Another by product of this pit was Fire Clay and also Ganister for making fire furnace bricks that were produced on site.
Bitchburn, Low Bitchburn, North Bitchburn and Howden Group of Collieries. These were situated at Howden le Wear, High Grange area and owned by the Bitchburn Coal Company. Cole was also produced and also brick pipes were made at the Bitchburn pipe yard.
Crook Colliery also known as Roddy Moor Colliery this pit also produced chemical by-products for paint and other products.
Woodifield Colliery the same named colliery also having a shaft at Crook. Produced coal and coke in abundance. The Colliery met the local needs and they also exported a great deal. Eventually the Colliery was closed then reopened again when it was renamed Steel House Pit. The latter four collieries all were situated on the north side of the River Gaunless:

COALS
FROM
CROOK COLLIERY.
S. & D. R. Co'S. WAY BILL.
16 day of Feb 1860

Waggon No.	Weight	Destination, and who for.
5256	4	Thos. Sanderson
11855	4	Wm Hopper
8061	4	John Hutchinson
9324	4	Wm Trumbull
5263	4	John Chaytor
4842	4	Darlington

EXPORT.
S. & D. R. CO'S WAY BILL.
OLD ETHERLEY COLLIERY,
(GEORGE PIT.)
5th day of July 186[illegible]

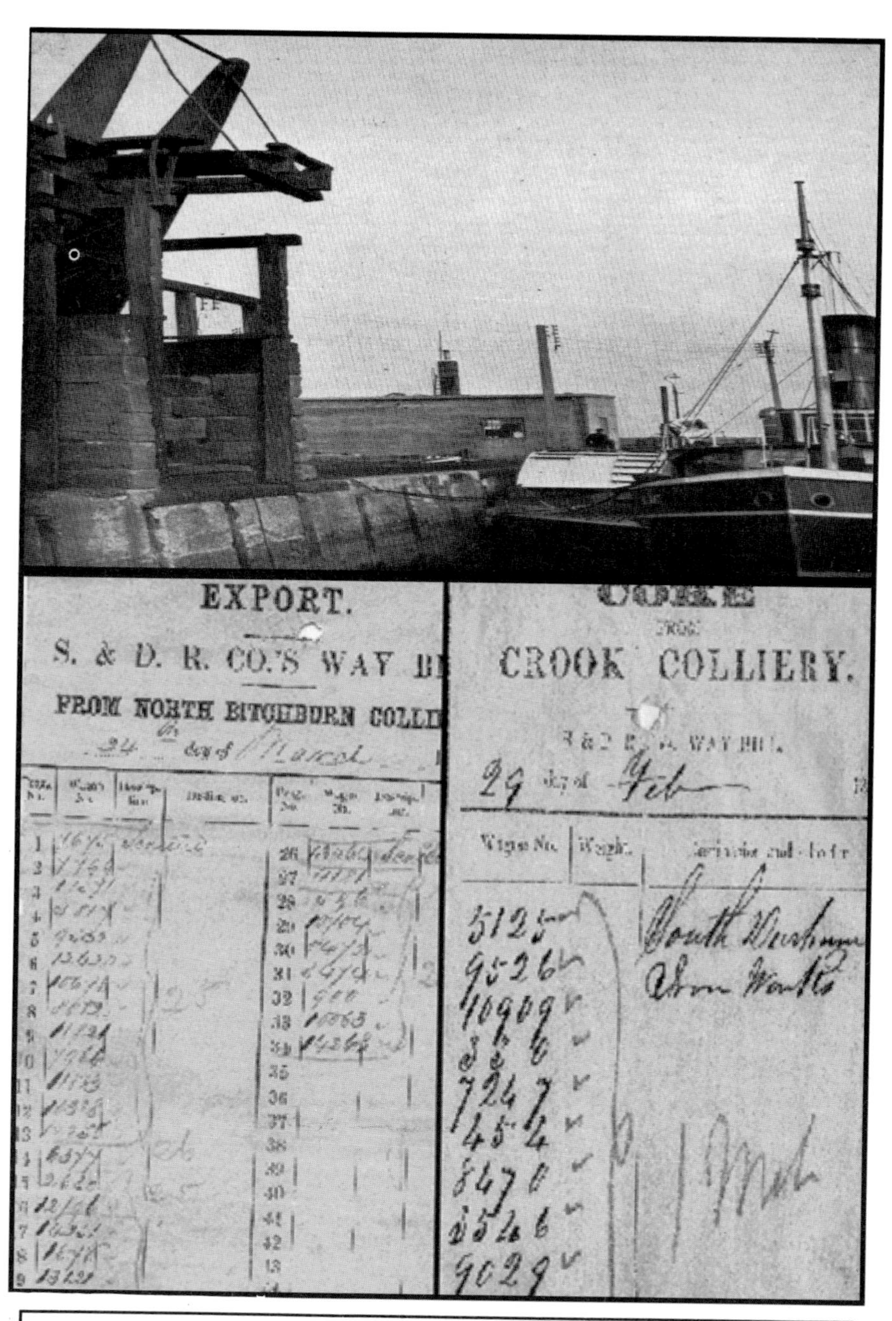

The export coal was then taken to Coal Drops around the Coastal areas; these particular drops were at Seaham Harbour, constructed about 1850

Randolph Colliery
The North Bitchburn Coal Company, sank the pit in 1893. The Brockwell was ventilated in 1893, by a 30 ft. Waddle fan, there were double Decker cages & there was also a Luthrig washer, and jigging screens, and also cocking was carried out in Coppee Ovens. Pease & Partners took over operations in 1927, but the Randolph Coal Company took over in 1933, after Nationalisation a new drift was driven in to the Hutton in 1953, the Pit finally closing in February 1962.

Etherley Colliery
The Pheonix Pit worked by Henry Stobart and Co. Old Etherley, in 1840s. There were also two other Etherley shafts, The George, (Escomb), The Jane, near Witton Park Iron Works. The Jane ceased operations, in between 1887-1897, and the George was disused between 1897-1920, the Jane was

Shildon Datton Colliery. Sunk on Surtees land and worked by Balckow & Vaughan. The Brockwell seam was worked, 5 feet 6 inches in this area. It yielded 800 tons each working day in the 1890s. Datton was active from 1830 to 1924. Apparently it acquired its name because of Irish Pitmen; when asked where they worked they replied " Dat', un". Was served by the Surtees Railway which was a branch off from the S&D Railway at Shildon station. Railway the Shildon Boy Scouts converted the Pit heap to a playing field on memory of the Boy Scouts.

Above a group of Shildon coal miners around 1912, there was a host of Collieries in the Shildon area, including Datton & Brussleton Colliery a short distance from Shildon towards Royal Oak, at the summit of the Brussleton incline:

cost affective. The 'National Coal Board', was formed in 1947 and at that time they owned eight of these Collieries leaving eight still under private ownership. Together they employed 2000 men and produced a half a million tons of coal a year.

By 1973 all on the 1947 list had closed leaving three private Collieries that employed 42 people and provided 16.000 tons of coal annually. Throughout the North of England a similar pattern emerged except for the North East Coastal Collieries that produced the reserves needed for any Power Stations remaining. At this time vast reserves were found in these collieries lying under the North Sea. With the reduction in mining interests in the Bishop Auckland, Shildon areas came massive changes to the Rail system that had successfully serviced the Collieries from the commencement of the S&D Railway. In later years employment was created by Shildon Shops and the Railway Yards in the West Auckland area:

S&D Progress Results

In the first year, 2.5% return was made on revenue of £9194, but there after it went from strength to strength. The second year (1826-7) £18,304, £14,455 was accounted for the carriage of coal. The equivalent figures in (1829-30) £23,727 and £20,951), and sufficient to pay a dividend of 5%. In (1826-7) 80,446, tons of coal had been carried on the line and in the year 1829-30, 147,570 tons. These figures were far in excess of the original estimate of Edward Pease and his associates. It was an amazing fact that between 1825-1830, the average price of a ton of coal at Stockton fell from 18 shillings to 8/6d; this was the end product of transport costs brought about by rail transportation of coal. Five years after the opening of S&D Railway, the role of the railways in Great Britain changed; trains were used to carry people and also freight between major cities. The London & Birmingham Railway opened in 1837-1838, classed as the first line to London. This had been a great feat of engineering.

Robert Stephenson

Arguably the greatest engineer of the times, he was the chief engineer of the project. The line had to climb the Chiltern Hills and also the Northamptonshire Hills crossing three rivers: the Thames, Avon and Ouse. Robert Stephenson plotted the route with precision, having gentle curves and easy gradients. Tunnels were expertly planned at Kilsby and Watford; deep-cuttings at Tring and Roade and the viaduct at Wolverton was added to make it a magnificent fete of engineering. Robert Stephenson had gained very important knowledge with the

Pease family and the S&D Railway; he remained great friends with the family throughout his life.

He also spent pleasurable periods visiting Edward at Darlington, where he stayed as a guest of Edward's, sampling the exquisite a la carte food and exotic fruits that the family were used to eating, and which were grown in Edward's garden. Robert and Edward sat talking until the early hours, mainly on his life's experiences to date, his adventures were amazing for his age and his conversation stimulated Edward. Robert's tubular bridge over the Menai Straits was a brilliant feat of engineering, as was the Royal Border Bridge at Berwick on Tweed. This was the England-Scottish east coast route, completed in 1850. Another amazing bridge credited to Robert Stephenson, was the Newcastle High Level Bridge; Robert kept the same gauge OD 4ft 8in that they had used in the early days at Hetton; even on the Liverpool and Manchester; later an extra half-inch was added for better clearance. In 1827, the Market price for shares in the S&D Railway was £160 this was up from £120. Edward Pease had seen his project extremely successful, and he now stepped

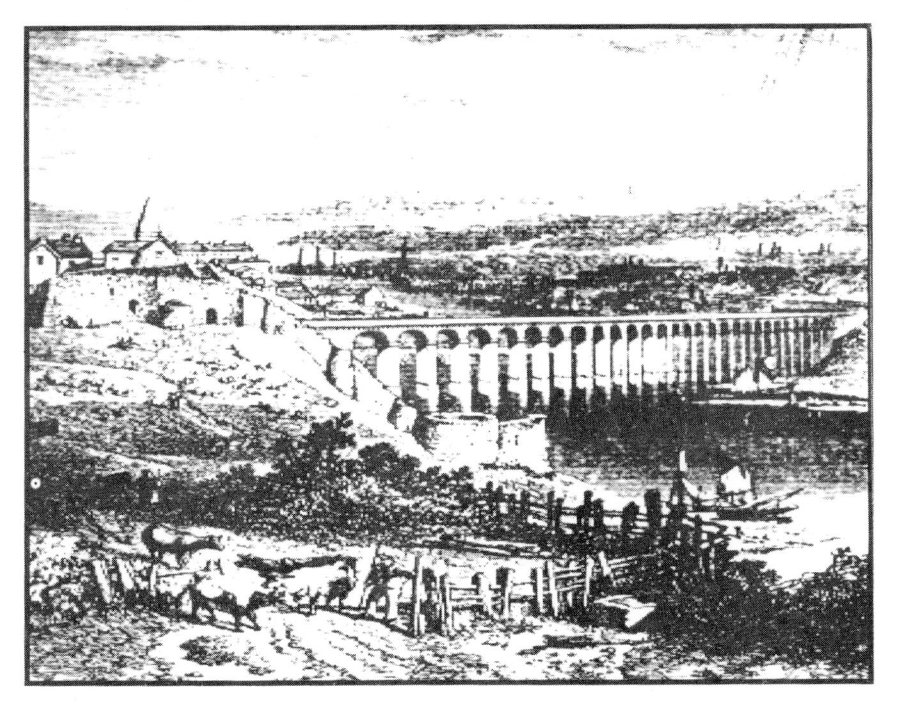

Royal Border Bridge at Berwick On Tweed, took Robert Stephenson three years to build:

Robert Stephenson's High Level Bridge at Newcastle upon Tyne:

Left popular photograph of George Stephenson; affectionately known as 'Geordie Stevy', in the North of England, he was uneducated being born when schools and education was just not available to the working man. George Stephenson surprised all of the sceptics by acting as Chief Engineer on many difficult projects, especially at 'Chat Moss' on his next project the Liverpool & Manchester Railway'. His natural knowledge of Surveying and Engineering skills were simply amazing:

Right Robert Stephenson; again he had natural ability. The difference with him and his father was "Education", his father made sure he was properly educated. Later in his life he was responsible for the erection of important bridges and again like his father his surveying skills were brilliant. Robert Stephenson could be compared with the greatest Engineers in the World and was as good as any at this time.

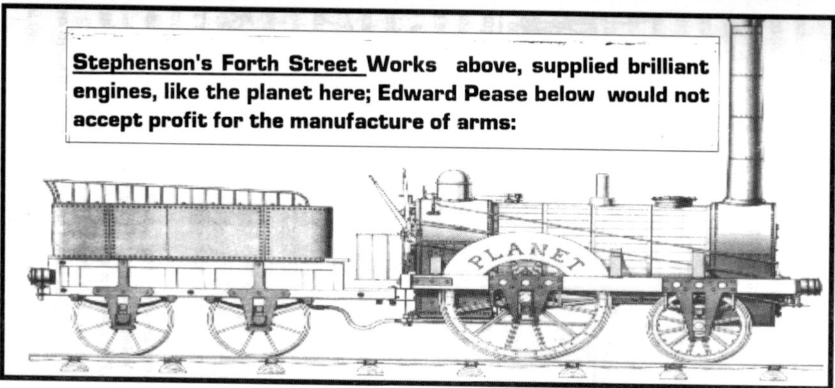

Stephenson's Forth Street Works above, supplied brilliant engines, like the planet here; Edward Pease below would not accept profit for the manufacture of arms:

George Stephenson left, Edward Pease right; even when there was a downturn in business Stephenson's made Edward Pease profit:

<u>Worlds Oldest Working Locomotive</u>; This picture was taken in 1901, the Locomotive was the oldest working Locomotive when the picture was taken in 1901 and built by George Stephenson for his Flag Ship Colliery Hetton. The Locomotive was evident at the S&D celebrations in 1925. It passed the grandstand where the future King & Queen of England King George V1 & Queen Elizabeth marvelled at the sight of the machine :Below an early chaldron wagon from the same period:

down, saying he would not enter a railway meeting again, and from then on Edward the Father of the Railways would devote the remainder of his life to the affairs of the Society of Friends. He regularly attended annual meetings in London and visited his many friends and relations. He remained in his residence at 73 Northgate, in Darlington Town Centre, where he looked after his greenhouse, his plums, apples and apricots. He was a lover of Port and wine and often entertained guests with Lisbon Madeira and Bucellas wines; he was nicknamed 'Neddy-Pease' by his many friends.

He was in deep mourning for years after the death of his wife in 1833, he was a 'flexible' Quaker, and mostly in business was a kind and considerate man. Edward Pease died in 1858 after a long life, fully earning his name as 'The Father of The Railways'. Most writers of the day showed that he earned this, and he was also very positive that locomotion Rail Transportation would pay its way in a period when it was badly needed

Joseph Pease

He was Edward's, second son, born on March 1799; he was married to Emma Gurney, co-heiress of Joseph Gurney, further tightening the Quaker links to the Darlington Stockton Railway. This led to the resignation of the present Chairman, Thomas Maynell, because of the Quaker monopoly of the Company affairs. Joseph was educated much the same as his father at Tathams in Leeds, completing his education at Joseph Foster, at Southgate, London, a Quaker school. As earlier, stated Joseph at 19 drew up the prospectus for the S&D Company.

By 1820 Joseph had a sound basis of expenditure for his business career. His father had left him a massive financial stake in the railroad, and Joseph was further inspired by his marriage to Emma Gurney. Unlike his father, Joseph was not affected in any way by an accumulation of wealth, and he very much went for it. Edward became a minister for the Society of Friends and also an elder, carrying on the family traditions. Joseph Pease knew the importance of coal, and in 1827 entered negotiations with Sir Thomas Claverine, of Durham regarding interests near Chester-le-Street, and it fell in line with the proposed expansion of the Stockton-Darlington railway. It was apparent that Stockton was not adapted for maximum exportation of coal, the river could only take small craft, and for this reason Middlesbrough was seen as the obvious transportation docks. Joseph also saw Middlesbrough as being the new shipping port for South West Durham Coal.

Quakers financed the necessary land for the project from the south of England, Thomas Richardson, Joseph Gurney, Henry Birkbeck, Simon Martin and Francis Gibson. Joseph Pease's contribution to the fund, of £35,000, was £7000 loaned by his father in Law, at a rate of interest of 4%, and this investment would be one of his most important. The site was a 520-acre estate, which would be developed into a busy seaport, which in time would also be a thriving iron-industry Port as well as coal. It was Joseph Pease's influence that got the finance and extra capital to erect the Wharfs at Middlesbrough, the money as stated above, coming from Thomas Richardson, Joseph Gurney (father in law) Henry Birkbeck, Simon Martin, Richard Hanbury Gurney. From 1821-1830 110,211 tons of coal was shipped from the Port, from 1831-1840 it increased to 8,293,984, then the following decade a figure of 17,019,714, this was a significant rise in the amount of coal shipped from the Tees. At the time there was opposition to the industry from the House of Lords, and mainly from Lords Londonderry and Durham, the reason for this was supposedly because of competition to their own coal industry. Norfolk Peers, Lord Dacks and Sheffield, as well as Lord Faversham, helped to get the Bill carried and Stockton people, for this reason, respected these Lords.

Joseph Gurney

There was also an attempt to tap the Stockton Darlington Railway at Simpasture near Shildon; this was to divert coal traffic to Port Clarence, fully endorsed by Parliament, later the same procedures were used, when the docks were erected at Hartlepool. The Pease Family were not easily put off. To prove that rail transport was a winner, Joseph purchased two collieries, initially St. Helens, then Adelaide. Other mine owners realised their mistake in not backing this mode of transport, but forever after were loyal to the Stockton Darlington Railway. A tunnel was put in 1300 yards westward, to transport coal from this area, which was bogged down by inclines and by stationary engines.

This same line was pushed on to Crook, then further on to the valley of Derwant at Consett. At the time Crook was almost virgin coal, the Wear Valley railway terminated at Frosterly, but later continued to Stanhope, and through extra, efforts, of Joseph continued on to Wearhead, this was promoted to supply limestone to Cleveland for the supply of Iron Ore. One of the contributing factors to the very large increase in the Tees Port, was the Tyne and Wear miners strike, in 1831 and it was estimated that this period had advanced the Tees coal industry in the London area by 20 years.

In the year 1833, Joseph Pease replaced Jonathan Backhouse, as treasurer of the Darlington-Stockton Railway, which was quickly followed by Joseph being appointed Chairman of the Management Committee. The successful project had a negative effect on the Clarence Railroad Scheme, which developed the north side of the Tees at Port Clarence. This was fronted by none other than Christopher Tennant (who wanted the Rushyford Auckland canal scheme) and it was dogged by problems. It was deeply in debt to the loan board, and they asked them to appoint a new board of directors. Joseph and Stockton-Darlington Railway was blamed for (in their words) 'ruining their closest competitor', when in fact the problem was managerial. The Clarence Railway, proposed a re-routing of their railway giving two different routes, but they were unsuccessful with both. It was ironic that Joseph Pease, as the representative for South Durham in Parliament, would be a member of the House of Commons Committee that was to reject both schemes by Clarence. This showed how ruthless and business like Joseph Pease could be, even though he was a devout Quaker. Joseph entered Parliament, and mainly represented his constituents, in their rights of agriculture, and commercial matters. His father rigorously campaigned for the abolition of the slave trade. J.S. Jeans in his Biography, made the following comments, on Joseph Pease,

"He was a speculator, doubtless, but he speculated wisely, and well. There was no gambling on his speculation, they were not determined on mere chance, or a fortuis, chain of events, although there was a certain rise in attending them, which he never shrank from undertaking, need we dwell on the splendour of his conceptions, and the still more splendid execution. The enterprise he led, their results, and they're rationale, the eminently practical character, and tendency of his genius. The impetus, which he gave to the railroad system, these and many other achievements, of his useful life, will find a permanent place in history, of his native town and country. As for his bounty, if not like that of Juliet, "As boundless as the sea", it was measured only by his means, and opportunities, he was an indiscriminative giver but, yet there are no really good

object that appealed to him in vain'. Between the years 1831-1835 the annual dividend for the Darlington-Stockton Railway was 6 to 8%, from 1835-1841 the dividend was 15% this was the highest of any. The other Companies, having to rely on passengers, when the Darlington-Stockton carried minerals, which was an advantage. Improvements had been made in 1854, to improve the channel of the river Tees, and improving the channel, of the river to the sea, from Stockton. A 'Joint Stock Company' was unable to find the finance for this improvement, for the benefit of the coal producers; the Admiralty nominated Joseph Pease, where he later became Chairman. The new commissioners, Messrs. Pease, father and son, Messrs. Bolckow, Vaughan, Richardson, and Hopkins, overcame the early difficulties.

The river had 3 feet of water at low tide and a 15 feet rise at high. Ships with 7000 tons of salt and iron on board, left the port for India and Japan. The discovery of salt aided the Port, and added to the general, trade available by deeper water. The value of the Darlington Stockton shares, which were originally, £100, was valued now at £260. By 1840 the largest shareholder was Thomas Richardson, having 141 shares, but by 1842 Joseph Pease was the largest shareholder, holding 239 shares. In a period of 20 years the Pease family owned 25% of the shares, and the original investment of £13,000 had rose to £60,000.

Edward Pease had been exactly right when he made his speech on Friday 13th November 1818, at Darlington Town Hall, when he estimated that 5% would be a minimum return on capital and that there was a high probability, of far more than this figure. The success pointed to sound management. Friday 13th November being a very lucky day for the Pease Family. At a census in 1831 in Middlesbrough the population was 154 in 1841 it increased to 5463 all people created by the extra work the railway brought. There were docks, warehouses, foundries, and churches, all created from the expansion that coal & Iron brought to the area.

Downturn

In 1842 the price of Scottish pig iron was £2 a ton, in 1846 it rose to £6 a ton, this was an enormous rise, and it affected manufacturers in a big way. The company had to ship iron ore from Whitby for the final stages of manufacture. The Clarence Railway started to use Hartlepool as a shipping port, resulting in the S&D Railway having to pay a penalty payment of £3000, which the company just could not afford. The period 1847-1851 was a severe crisis time for Pease and the Stockton-

Middlesbrough showed amazing development , top showing the 'Ship Inn', at the front of Stockton Street,; below the Tees from **Port Clarence** showing the coal staithes erected along the river bank allowing the Colliers to be loaded, from a painting completed in 1840:

Middlesbrough

Joseph Pease

Arthur Pease

The Transformation of Middlesbrough, initially a small farm bought by Joseph Pease and developed into a busy seaport. Joseph Pease was the largest Coal owner in the North East and became the first Quaker MP, to enter the Commons on Feb. 8th. 1833. The third son of Arthur Pease also entered the Commons in 1895

Port Darlington 1830

Darlington Railway; the Pease family were under serious financial strain. Edward as early, as 1846, noted in his diary that, from their Collieries and woollen mills, and also railways, there was no income forthcoming at all. Both Joseph and younger brother Henry received financial help from their brother-in-law, Francis Gibson, and Henry Birkbeck. Following the failure of the Union Bank, in Newcastle in October 1847, Edward reluctantly agreed to sustain Joseph's credit as treasurer, to the Stockton Darlington Railway, by giving him an unlimited guarantee.

At the end of 1849, Edward's shares were de-valued by not less than thirty or even forty thousand pounds, and shares once valued at £360, were now selling at £30, property once worth £60,000 now being worth £3,000. Joseph's health deteriorated, with the threat of bankruptcy in the year 1847, he suffered insomnia and with it depression. In the early months of 1849, the first symptoms of glaucoma, affected him, this would lead to total blindness later in life. There were two good happenings that lifted his spirits about this time. First, in 1846 he had joined his father in Robert Stephenson & Co. and his share of the profits was £7,000, this was set on prices prior to the recession. Second, the demand for coke had risen and at his collieries in the Auckland coalfields, up to 500 coke ovens worked happily away. In June, 1850, John Vaughan and Bolckow discovered major Ironstone deposits at Eston, on the north facing side of Cleveland Hills, near Middlesbrough, they had discovered the main seam at a point at its thickest.

In 1850 Bolckow and Vaughan sent, 4,000 tons of ironstone, to their Witton Park furnaces. The following year 188,000 tons were produced by the partnership, the effect made on The Stockton-Darlington Company was amazing. By the end of 1851 they were able to pay the guaranteed rents to the Middlesbrough, and Redcar, and Wear Valley railways, and also discharged all of the arrears. The Cleveland ore contained a high amount of silica and needed large amounts for fluxing, this also generated extra work. The Stockton Darlington had good cause to be optimistic; their rail system touched the very edge of the ironstone find, and a further fifty miles on the same line, the main iron works. £10,000 a year was added to the pockets of the company. Gladstone visited Middlesbrough in 1861 saying *that "Middlesbrough was 'the youngest child of England's enterprise" "It is an infant, but an infant Hercules"*. On the year of Gladstone's visit half a million tons of pig iron was produced on Teesside, by 1867 one million tons. In 1873, 2

Henry William Ferdinand Bolckow :

John Vaughan:

Marton Hall; Bolckow's home; below Gunnergate Hall; the home of John Vaughan:

million tons and a third of the total British output. In 1873 it produced 5½ million tons, it also had 90 blast furnaces. Pease and Co. awoke a sleeping giant, this remark was made by Samuel Smiles in 1856, that "*anybody who devotes himself body and soul can scarcely fail to make himself rich*", very little brains will do, this was certainly the case with iron ore.

Prime Minister Gladstone

A proposal for a rail link between Darlington and Barnard Castle was now coming to pass. Joseph Pease had authorised surveys, for a possible line as early as 1833, but it did not get off the ground until 1844, when the carpet and shoe manufacturers of Barnard Castle, joined forces with Darlington & Stockton Company. There was an objector to the scheme and that was Henry Vane, the second Duke of Cleveland, who, like his father before him, was very protective of his way of life. In a public interview with Joseph Pease, he had spoken of the excellence of the turnpike road, when it was known that it was not satisfactory for transport. Joseph Pease remarked to the meeting "you see the man you have to deal with, beyond his own interests he has no feeling."

All discussion was in vain, but the committee and Joseph Pease, thinking that the Duke's opposition to the bill may have mellowed, again revived it in 1852. New proposals were put on the table in that, maintenance would only be charged at half the cost and this would also be the case with haulage, until the profit or dividend reached 4%. Joseph also agreed that the Darlington & Stockton would meet the subscription of the project, which amounted to £22,000.

A Bill of Incorporation was drawn up and considered by the House of Commons in May 1853. The Duke of Cleveland again opposed the Bill saying that it was the device of a scheming artful individual, trying to deceive the people of Barnard Castle for his own benefit, since it would reduce the cost of the transportation of coal and other goods, along the Tees Valley, from the Peases Collieries. Joseph Pease even suggested an alternative scheme showing that this was not the case, but to no avail and it was rejected in June that year. Again a renewed application for an alternative route was put forward in the autumn of that year by two solicitors, with a representative of West Hartlepool, led by Ralph Ward Jackson, who said that it was the aim of Joseph Pease to control automatically the entire district. Reminiscent of Graham Tennant and is *Prima Facia* evidence of the fact. Joseph always had a good reputation for being very sincere and of having purity of motive.

By the autumn of 1853, the Duke of Cleveland was whipping up Pease phobia, which could have intensified when the Darlington Barnard Castle line was approved in May 1854. The grounds for the project to succeed was that it offered very few engineering problems and it was strongly backed by the people of Barnard Castle. The line actually opened in July 1856. The Duke of Cleveland attended the opening ceremony, he expressed his hope that differences with the Pease Family would be forgotten, but cynics noted that he was permitted to nominate a director for life. From 1841 to 1865 Joseph Pease, devoted himself to educational and social, reforms. In 1865 he became completely blind, but continued works of humanity as best he could. This was not confined to England; he declined an honour from Spain, of the 'Grand Cross of Charles II.' for his efforts for the moral advancement of the Spanish people. It appears that in the year 1850 two separate companies were established because of the extra mine activity.

Joseph Pease and Partner

was concerned with the colliery side of the business, this together with coke ovens, and firebricks. These interests were Adelaide, St. Helens nr Bishop Auckland, Tindale, Sunnyside, Peases West, Bowden Close, Stanley and Wooley, near Crook, Esh-Winning, Waterhouses, Ushaw Moor, Brandon, Windlestone Colliery, Chilton nr Ferryhill. In 1870 the total output was more than 1 million tons, one third of which was converted to coke for smelting proposes.

J.W. Pease and Company,

Were concerned with the largest Producers of ironstone, in Cleveland, with an output of approx. 1 million tons annually total Cleveland production in 1872 being 6.3 million tons, the wage bill alone in this department was £100,000 a year.

J & J W. Pease

Was a successor to the Peases Bank of the 18th Century, the Banking section was re-established in the time of Joseph Whitwell Pease, and was basically the counting house of the Pease companies, including the Darlington Stockton Railway. After 1863 it became local banker to the NER and the Consett Iron Company.

Death of Joseph Pease

Joseph Pease died in the year 1872 a very wealthy man; an outside estimate of his estate at the time of this was £320,000, 3 times more than the typical Victorian businessman. This was because of the never-ending effort Joseph put into everything he did, both as a Mine owner and a railway promoter, opening up the Cleveland mineral wealth, and backing many or even any worthwhile business for the good of posterity and his fellow man. His funeral was on 19th February 1872. All commercial premises closed in Darlington; flags flew at half-mast at all NER Stations. Words were hard to describe such an amazing business man as Joseph Pease, and Reverend Henry Kendall described him as well as any one could, he said: "*Joseph was one who's substance was mines and merchandise, and roads and horses of iron and very extensive possessions, so that this man was the greatest of all men of the North East of England.*" Joseph's sons were now on their own. They were Joseph Whitwell Pease, Edward, Arthur, Gurney, and Charles. Joseph senior had high hopes for his oldest son, Joseph Whitwell; he hoped he could carry on the Dynasty where he left off. Like Edward before him, Joseph Whitwell had to start from the bottom; at the age of 17 he entered the family counting house as a clerk, to learn bookkeeping. After the merger

Guisborough Railway Station, opened in 1853, backed by S&D Railways. The station brought all of the fresh produce to run Hutton Hall the home of the Peases. The station was situated very near to the Hall;

Sir Joseph Whitwell Pease:

of 1863, as a member of 'Darlington Stockton', he joined the board of the NER on behalf

Barnard Castle Railway Station after years of wrangling Joseph Pease at last managed to extend the rail network to Barnard Castle:

of the family. The future of the Pease Dynasty was in his hands.

Sir Joseph Whitwell Pease

Joseph's eldest son born in 1828, and the right hand of his father. As his father's strength failed after 1850, he took on the ever-growing responsibility he inherited. One of 8 brothers, most of who died prematurely, leaving him relatively on his own to carry the burden of the whole of the family's public and private business. In 1852 Joseph Whitwell became Director of Barnard Castle Railway, his father also became a Director, then they were joint treasurers, the Railway after this went from strength to strength. In 1852-3 a private company was formed to develop the newly found iron-ore deposits, extended the railway to Guisborough. Joseph and his son acted as guarantors. The Railway was subject to a fierce attack in Parliament. In one session alone it was in committee stage 23 days in the House of Commons.

Barnard Castle Railway

This railway was extended to Torbay and Penrith, with the motivation of the Pease's. It was actually down to Henry Pease, who secured this final link between east and west coast. The last remaining section was Saltburn-on-Sea, which also owes the Pease family, and Joseph in particular, for its existence. The extension to Tebay opened up the market for Durham coke, to the west coast, where it was badly needed for smelting the rich hematite ore, of the western mines of Cumberland and Westmoreland.

Consett Railway

In 1857 there was great panic in the North East of England. The Coside (Consett) Iron Company, were large debtors of the S&D, Railway and also of the Northumberland and Durham

Bank, who stopped payment. Sir Joseph Pease (then Mr) took the Company in hand, a new Company was formed, and there was great difficulties with the liquidation of the old Company. Joseph Pease, and Co. received substantial aid from the old Gurney connection, and also from the Bankers Messrs. Drewett and Fowler, (grandfather of Mrs. Alfred Pease). There was also troubles at Middlesbrough, the Peases being responsible for establishing, the iron-ore business. The Peases had also encouraged Mr Bolckow and Mr Vaughan, giving them easy terms for land and also letters of introduction, which was a great help.

Bolckow, and Vaughan, had established works at Witton Park, near Bishop Auckland, and they were in serious financial trouble and their Bankers had placed the Sheriff's officers bailiffs in their works, the Peases came to their rescue. Joseph Whitwell Pease went to their Bankers, and had the Bailiffs removed. Securities were raised and deposited with the Peases, until the iron-ore, made their works profitable again. Many years later Joseph again came to their rescue and this time preventing a Catastrophe. The Peases had, over this period, with the help of others, created Middlesbrough with a local railway system, they had constructed the Dock area, saved the iron industry for the people of Middlesbrough, and opened the West Durham Coalfield, turned Middlesbrough into a credible port, brought in other industries such as potteries, (managed by, Isaac Wilson). Up to this date no railways existed between Darlington and York, the 4-horse coach was still in regular use.

Again finance had to be arranged privately, and the Peases, again with their Southern relatives from Norfolk and London, had to arrange this. At one of these branch meetings, Mr. Samuel Gurney said to Joseph, "*Joseph, that railway of thine will beggar thee.*" "*That entirely depends on the kindness of my friends,*" Joseph replied, The Darlington York railway was completed on time. In 1854 was the year of the great amalgamation, all of the Companies came together under the North Eastern Railway. In 1863 the Stockton and Darlington, joined this alliance, and 4 members placed on its board, Messrs. Joseph Whitwell Pease, Henry Pease, Alfred Kitching, Colonel Stobart. In 1865 the Newcastle, Carlisle and Hartlepool, also added to the union. Sir J. Lowthian Bell became Chairman, of the Locomotive Committee, and later, Deputy Chairman of the Board. Sir Joseph W. Pease, became Chairman, of the traffic company, and later, Chairman, of the Board, and since 1894, Chairman. Sir David Dale became Chairman, of the Works Committee, Mr. Henry Tennant, who had been accountant, to the Great Northern Company, then to the United Company, became, General Manager and later Director. It was interesting that in the present day Railtrack made an announcement on Friday May 28th. 1999 that they made £425 million profit in their yearly returns, 'Rail Track' also published a ten year 27 billion investment programme.

Early Family Life

The Pease family home prior to 1850 was Woodlands, on the western edges of Darlington. Darlington being Quaker dominated was populated to approximately 12,000 people. The Quaker families at the time were the Peases, and Backhouses, the latter being bankers, with premises at High Row, Darlington. Joseph Pease having a family of 6 boys, 4 girls, being a total family of 10. By 1880, 3 boys had died leaving Joseph Whitwell (born1828), Edward, (born1834), Arthur, (born, 1837), 4 sisters, remained, 2 of which, were married.

Marriage of cousins, Henry Fell and Elizabeth Pease, in 1862

The marriage celebrations of the above were a very lavish affair, and these were only cousins. Thirty Carriages left the bride's home, North Lodge, for the Meeting House, and on their return, the guests were treated to a magnificent Banquet containing the following *asparagus soup, oyster soup a la reine, soup a la julienne, turkeys, raised ham and veal pies, pigeon pies, boars head, and ducklings of lamb; spring chickens, and boiled fouls, lobster salads, pressed beef and guinea fouls, aspic of eels, of salmon and shrimps; prawns; and sweets to follow, included six kinds of creams, five sorts of jellies, pastries, meringues, hedge hog, hen's nest, cakes fruit and ices, with non-alcoholic drinks, including temperance champagne.* It was said that these occasions were rare:

The couple visited France on their honeymoon, they went to Paris, Tours, Bordeaux, Bayonne, and Biarritz, afterwards returning to their newly built mansion at Brinkburn, built by Joseph Pease, and Partners, built with buff coloured brick, backing onto large grounds, near, Pierremont, the home of the groom's father. On the day of the wedding 700 workers at Henry Pease & Co Mills, enjoyed a railway excursion, to Redcar, where a saxhorn band, which went with them, & entertained them.

The Pease's also had a home in Guisborough, called Hutton Hall; Joseph Sn. took his family there for a monthly holiday every year. Joseph also had the shooting rights for the surrounding area. Alfred pleasantly remembered the summer evenings, at the house. In 1862, Joseph bought, an estate, at Pinchinthorpe, 2 miles, to the west of Guisborough, Hutton Hall and this estate, totalled, 2700 acres. For all of this, home was still very much Woodlands at Darlington. Joseph Peases London home was Princess Gardens, later they bought a very classy house at 24, Kensington Palace Gardens, London. Joseph obviously spent, time here relaxing after a hard day in Parliament, especially, when lobbying, for new rail projects. For some time now Joseph had intended moving his whole family to Hutton Hall, he quite enjoyed the country life, where he could indulge in country pursuits, free from business pressures and politics.

Alfred Pease, had very definite, views about his family's involvement, in industry, saying, *"I disliked from childhood, the spoiling industrial hand of my family, who thought they were always doing good work, in providing more and more, employment for people. I could see as a boy, that the more that they did this the more families of boys would be produced for whom more and more, mines and pits, and factories, would have to be made, till our lovely world, would be ash heaps, chimneys, and hideous houses under smoke clouds".* In 1882 Joseph Whitwell Pease, was offered a Baronetcy by the Prime Minister of the time, Gladstone, which after consultation with the rest of the family he accepted, saying, at least it was some public recognition for past members of the family in what they had achieved.

Hutton Old Hall

The Hall was the charm of antiquity, old gardens, in a sweet corner of the Cleveland Hills. The gardens were old world, the nursery door, and window opened on to a rose garden, York, Lancaster, Gloria Mundi, old fashioned roses, interspersed with little box edged beds of Verbena, Blue Salvia, and such things. The side of the house was half covered by an enormous, Jargon Elle, Pear Tree, the leaves of which flopped against, the window of the bedroom, in which Joseph Whitwell and his brother Jack slept.

Hutton Hall (Modified)

By the time Joseph bought the Hall, he made sweeping changes, to the Old Hall. By 1867, the old cornfields, and Whiney pastures, were laid into a park, the old hedgerows disappeared, and fine roads took the place of old lanes and bridle paths, bridges

Hutton Hall, above as described earlier was situated at the heart of prime forest and agricultural land. The House headed a small village & the air was so good it was always referred to as 'Alpine Village'. The delightful scenery was a pleasure to see. The Peases used the Hall as a Country retreat; where they could be far away from the extreme pressures of Business: Left the impressive billiard room

Above 'Pinchinthorpe House', Sir Alfred Pease lived here; he was a well known Sportsman /Author. Below the 'Cleveland Hills as seen from Great Ayton. The hills that gave the Pease family a lifeline after the downturn in business in 1860. Bolckow and Vaughan discovered Iron Ore right on their doorstep; virtually yards from their Railway.

STOCKTON & DARLINGTON RAILWAY COACHES.

The SUMMER ARRANGEMENTS will cease on the 30th Instant, and the Trains run the same as last season until further notice: viz.—

Winter Arrangements, commencing October 1st, 1840.

ST. HELEN'S AUCKLAND TO DARLINGTON.

First Trip - - at half-past Eight o'Clock.
Second Trip - - at One -
Third Trip - - at Five -

DARLINGTON TO ST. HELEN'S AUCKLAND.

First Trip - - at half-past Eight o'Clock.
Second Trip - - at One -
Third Trip - - at Five -

DARLINGTON TO STOCKTON.

Merchandize Train - at half-past Six o'Clock.
First Class Train - - at half-past Nine -
Merchandize Train - at Eleven -
First Class Train - - at Two -
Merchandize Train - at Four -
First Class Train - - at Six -

STOCKTON TO DARLINGTON.

First Class Train - at 10 min. bef. Eight o'Clock.
Merchandize Train at 10 min. bef. Nine -
First Class Train - at 20 min. past Twelve -
Merchandize Train at 20 min. past Two -
First Class Train - at 20 min. past Four -
Merchandize Train at 20 min. past Six -

STOCKTON TO MIDDLESBRO'.

First Trip - at Eight o'Clock.
Second do - - at Nine -
*Third do - at Ten -
Fourth do - - at Eleven -
Fifth do - at half-past Twelve -
Sixth do - at half-past One -
*Seventh do - at half-past Two -
Eighth do - - at half-past Three -
Ninth do - at half-past Four -
Tenth do - - at half-past Five -
*Eleventh do - at a quarter bef. Seven -

MIDDLESBRO' TO STOCKTON

*First Trip - at half-past Seven o'Clock.
Second do - - at half-past Eight -
Third do - at half-past Nine -
Fourth do - - at half-past Ten -
*Fifth do - at Twelve -
Sixth do - - at One -
Seventh do - at Two -
Eighth do - - at Three -
*Ninth do - at Four -
Tenth do - - at Five -
Eleventh do - at Six -

* Are in connexion with the first class Trains to and from Darlington.

Tickets must be taken at least Five Minutes before the Trains start.

NO SMOKING ALLOWED IN ANY OF THE COMPANY'S COACHES.

MARKET COACHES.

A Coach and Cattle Carriage will leave St. Helen's Auckland, on Mondays, at half-past Six o'Clock; and Shildon, at Seven in the Morning.

HORSES, CATTLE, AND CARRIAGES, CAREFULLY CONVEYED BETWEEN STOCKTON AND DARLINGTON, BY THE MERCHANDIZE TRAINS:

Horse, [illegible]—Gig, [illegible] or Horse and Gig, [illegible]—Four-wheeled Carriage, [illegible], or with Two Horses, [illegible]—Horned Cattle, [illegible] each.—Sheep, [illegible] each, or [illegible] per Score.—Dogs, [illegible] each.

If by the FIRST CLASS Train, Horse [illegible]—Gig, [illegible]—Horse and Gig, [illegible]—Four-wheeled Carriage, [illegible], or with Two Horses, [illegible]

Railway Office, Darlington, September [illegible], 1840.

COATES AND FARMER, PRINTERS, HIGH ROW, DARLINGTON.

replaced fords and stepping stones.

New Hall

Built in Domestic Gothic Style, brick dressed in stone. The architect was Alfred Waterhouse, the Architect who designed the 'Natural History Museum', London. The house had 2 halls, a billiard room, 5 reception rooms, 5 bathrooms, a conservatory, a winter garden, and ninety-one feet in length, and a central tiled walk, with fernery. Cellars were reached by 3 staircases; Turkish bath's with tiled and marbled walls, and floors, cooling room, weighing room, furnace room, and wine and beer cellars. Grounds and gardens were laid out with weeping elm and Cedar of Lebanon, clumps of Rhododendrons and other flowering shrubs, and had a broad terraced walk that led to the Italian Garden. Stabling for 24 horses, Booth's House, Head Gardener's house, Coachman's House, 13 greenhouses, 7 of which were free standing, these later produced, grapes, melons, oranges, bananas, pineapples, figs, apricot's, peaches, nectarines, plums, and pears.

A miniature lake was produced called the pond, stocked with trout, and also complimented with a boathouse, and a tearoom above it. All cleverly installed into 54 acres of private grounds. Twenty gardeners were employed, and just as many house servants. Joseph had arranged for the Railway Station to be built at the end of the drive. The railway was handy in many ways for the Whitwell Pease's, who lived off the fat of the land. Sausages were imported from Cornwall, fish came by train from York, fruit came from where ever it was available, nectarines, peaches, apricots, melons, grapes, and York hams were all specially bought and were included on daily menus. Regular trips for the children, during their holidays, to Falmouth where they had their steam yacht '*Rosemary*' birthed.

This is all due to accumulated wealth, over the years, and quite contrary to Quaker beliefs, and also the advice given by Edward some years ago, himself a very wealthy man, 'He always advised containment in matters of this kind'. A sharp contrast at the time was when his pitmen were treated to a meal on the occasion of the birthday of grandson, Joseph Whitwell Pease, and the following account was entered in Francis Newborns diary. 'On Monday 26th, all pitmen in the employment of Joseph Pease were entertained in a field adjoining Adelaide Colliery; 1,600 sat down, Mr. and Mrs. Joseph Pease and 11 children also sat down. There were speeches after dinner; music was played; yet on other occasions like horticulture shows, no music was allowed.

Success in business showed in the quality housing that was owned by the Pease family, top to bottom; Southend built by Edward Backhouse (1781-1860; Joseph Pease later bought it. Edward Pease spent many hours here with his grand-children. Pierremont, Henry Pease owned (1807-1888). Polam Hall, bought by Johnathan Backhouse jun. (1778-1842) in later years was to become a respected High School for girls.

The massive Public Library in Crown Street, left to the Darlington people by the Peases; the author has spent many pleasurable hours here.

APPENDICES

A. COMPANIES ABSORBED BY THE STOCKTON AND DARLINGTON RAILWAY

NAME OF COMPANY	INDEPENDENT EXISTENCE
MIDDLESBROUGH AND REDCAR	1845 - 1858
WEAR VALLEY	1845 - 1858
MIDDLESBROUGH AND GUISBOROUGH	1852 - 1858
DARLINGTON AND BARNARD CASTLE	1854 - 1858
EDEN VALLEY	1858 - 1862
FROSTERLEY AND STANHOPE	1861 - 1862
SOUTH DURHAM AND LANCASHIRE	1857 - 1862

The Stockton and Darlington Railway Company was amalgamated in 1863 with the North Eastern Railway Company".

The dinner consisted of bread, beef, and ale. There were 500

Joseph Whitwell Pease (1828-1903) with his family:

mugs, and at the end of the day only 70 remained intact, after the pitmen amused themselves by throwing them at each other. The Peases from minerals alone supplied The North Eastern, Railway with revenue of approximately £1000 a day. Since Sir Joseph Pease's death, one of his Companies, Pease and Partners, have paid North Eastern Railways, £9 million Sterling in Railway dues alone, £250,000, to £400,000 into the coffers of the Company, and this being just one of his industries. In 1865-1903, the Peases produced many amenities for the people of Durham County, among which are schools, miners hospitals, mechanics' and miners' institutes, convalescing homes, libraries, assembly rooms.

Sir Joseph Pease has supported the Miners Permanent Fund, railways, and other superannuating funds, and his family also have done something for their hometown, Darlington. His father Edward gave Darlington Municipal Buildings, and a Market Place, and also a Free Library. North Road, cemetery, and many other gifts, Almshouses have also been founded by the Peases in the town. Here ends the story of a very remarkable Darlington Family, who not only funded the Railways, but also persisted through one major problem after another, until the railways were fully established. Not only Darlington, Stocktoh, and Middlesbrough, but all of the North of England, must be very proud to be associated with the Pease family.

EDWARD PEASE
DIARIES

Edward made daily visits, to his wife's grave, when he was at Darlington, he absolutely adored her living, and in death. He was consoled by the fact that he may join her in death when his time came. I was amazed at Edward's innermost concern, not only to his family, but also for his fellow Quakers and his fellow man. He worried constantly about his sons, mainly Edward and Joseph, regarding their health, both had problems with various complaints, Edward would die prematurely, while Joseph eventually would go blind. Edward always referred to all his family especially Joseph as 'dear Joseph', and constantly referred to his brilliant mind. During this period, transport was in its early stages, Edward travelled, extensively, not only throughout this county, but also throughout the country and the world, mostly staying with other members of the Society of Friends.

Before concentrating on Edward's diaries, I intend to note a few customary rules of the Quaker Religion.

Dress

There was attention to great simplicity; they refused to change with fashion. Mainly drawn from the middle class, they wore simple clothing. If gaily-clothed people joined the Society, they had to lay aside their gaudy clothing.

Furniture & Decoration

They always attempted to be simple; the richer ones used the best of articles, mainly because they stood the test of time. Things like bright coloured curtains and fashionable, furniture, along with pictures and photographs were frowned upon.

Speech

'Thou', takes the place of 'You', 'Thee', was also a regular saying, the following was also avoided in speech, 'Saint', 'Christian name', 'Good Bye', 'Reverend', and all other titles of courtesy. Joseph Pease, found great difficulty, with these rules, when in Parliament but managed to get through.

Head Covering

When praying, they did so,

The small simple <u>Friends</u> grave yard behind the meeting Hall in Skinnergate, Darlington, I have visited here often and was amazed at the simplicity & humility of it all from in life very rich and powerful families.; below <u>Edward Pease</u> also his grave stone as noted :

The Friends meeting hall in Skinnergate Darlington:

uncovered, they would not use the same outward mark of homage for men as they would for God, wearing their hats, in meetings for worship, in courts of law, churches, and in the presence of kings. They never doffed them as a sign of honour or respect to man or place. Being a protest against extravagant fashions or dress, in that man was more in the presence of God, in one place than another.

Marriage

Before a marriage had taken place, the man had to publicly declare his intention of marriage, producing certificates of consent, from his fiancée, and her parents. A deputation of 2 men and 2 woman would be appointed to visit the parties, making sure that they were quite 'clear', from other engagements, and they reported back at the next meeting. All parties then signed a declaration form if indeed they were found to be 'clear' and free to marry. In the case of a second marriage, the rights of the children are in the care of the meeting.

It has only recently been changed that the friends could only marry other friends, and any variation from this meant disownment. One of the advantages of this rule was said to be discipline, where a mixed marriage may cause problems, with this, a marriage within the rules would not. Woman were found to be disowned more than men, in that woman were found to be easily distracted by the fashions of the world. Marriage to first cousins was forbidden and this rule effected numbers within the Society with the frequency of disownment

Funerals

All unnecessary mourning was discouraged, and there was no ceremonial pomp allowed. Mourning clothing was never worn, and there were no rites observed at the burial; a meeting was held subsequently, to the internment. Usually at the graveside a prayer is said by one of the friends. Prior to modern times, families buried their dead in gardens, or orchards. Headlam Hall the residence, of Mr. Joseph A. Pease, had many family buried there. It was not until later years that gravestones were permitted, no epitaphs, and certainly no ornamental gravestones. Honouring the dead, according to Quakers, was remembering them as they lived, their good works, and achievements

Occupations

A few were Doctors, some Sea Captains, and Solicitors, most lived in the country, as far away as possible from the temptations of city life, but requiring facilities for common worship and education. These days these facilities are mainly available in the towns, therefore a high influx of Quakers are situated in towns.

Earlier Friends warned their comrades about the manufacture of arms and slave trading in the towns, was strictly forbidden. During the 1914-18 war, many men refused to take up arms, were branded as cowards, and summarily shot, indeed men were imprisoned at Richmond Castle, for being Conscientious Objectors, they were returned to France where they were executed. Some must have come from the ranks of the Quakers. Modern day rational thinking, in 1999, gave these men pardons, recognising the fact that they were indeed, Conscientious Objectors.

The Poor

All members of the Society, in theory, are bound to support each other, all members can seek, and expect, support as members of one big family. In London, a committee was formed to consider the needs of the poor, relief is given very privately. Subscriptions are taken quarterly especially for this relief, making sure that they did not fall into the pauper class of society. All forms of gambling were frowned upon; their reason being that it disturbed the mind and led to misery.

Music

Music was not allowed at all, thinking it led to self-gratification, and that it would also disturb the retirement of the elder member of the society. Theatres were strictly forbidden, the reason given for this, the stage caused corrupt morals. George Fox, William Penn, and Robert Barclay banned it all together, saying it was a comedy of the mind.

Dancing

This was forbidden because it led to vain amusement, and frivolity. Timothy Hackworth and his family loved dancing but this was strictly, kept to the privacy of his home, as noted earlier.

Discipline of the Society

There are discipline meetings convened each quarter. The extreme punishment being disownment. Cases are judged on immorality, drunkenness, marrying a first cousin, or outside the Society, swearing, insolvency, breach of rules, etc.

In a previous story Jeremiah Dixon, fell foul to the drinking to excess, rule and it was reported to the society, when it was entered in the meeting minutes.

Edward Pease was born in the house of his parents, Joseph and Mary Pease, at Darlington. The house is still standing, and is today, the offices of solicitors. The garden has disappeared and the whole town has grown around it. It is a simple red brick, red tiled, house, situated a short walk from the Market Place.

Edward had a very long life and could remember, happenings from years ago, especially, when talking to grandchildren. He clearly remembered talking to people who could recall Culloden in 1746, especially an old lady who helped to knit the woollen waistcoats for the Hanoverian troops passing through with the Duke of Cumberland's army.

In his later years, Edward concentrated mainly on the administration of The Society, visiting members, in other parts of the country and even abroad. He kept very interesting diaries, regarding his movements over this period. There were many Hotel bills and vouchers, which showed that Edward was partial to the consumption of his fair share of liquid refreshment, which included: ale, spirits, and wine. Edward's family were brought up having ale with their meals, he carried this practice out all of his life. One Hotel Bill in particular was from 'The Kings Head' Richmond, in 1808. Dinner, 17/6, Ale & Beer, 5/11, Sherry & Lisbon, 5/6, Wine & Nagus, 15/-, Brandy, Rum, & Gin, 9/-, Horse Hay & corn bag 5/-.

The Diaries

All of the diaries prior to 1838 were destroyed, the diaries which are available are for the last 20 years, recorded when Edward was 71 years of age, in 1838, continuing until, his 92nd year, the diary for 1852, appears to be missing.

The following are parts of Edward's diary, as noted.
I have neither edited or corrected any of Edwards notes, they are as he wrote them:

Journey Abroad in the anti Slavery Cause:

1824

Sixth 6th.mo, -

I left London, in company with cousins, Josiah & Rachel Forster, the latter about to commence her visit her friends in Kent. The road, from London to Rochester, in many parts, in sight of the Thames, was strikingly beautiful, the day was cool and gloomy, and my situation not of choice on the outside, I was separated from the interesting society of my friends. We were kindly received by W. Rickman, where my companions lodged, while I was similarly accommodated at R. Horsnaill's with much hospitality, and from the friends received much attention.

We called to see Mr. R.L. Weston, who has upwards of fifty, received in his school; the premises and house are well adapted to the establishment, and the general appearance of things as well as the Friend and his accommodation much exceeded those of H.F.S. the cost of house and garden was £2500, and I think the £800 more in the erection of an excellent, school room, etc., had been expended. The sight of their instruction and the reflection of so many of our youth receiving a guarded and religious, education yielded a very pleasing reflection on my mind.

Sixth Month 1824 In Paris

The Jesuits at this moment are taking steps after the example of the Bible Society, to raise funds to be applied to any purpose to oppose any circulation of the scriptures, collecting a 1d a week from each individual, and where every one who yet approved of such opposition and could not pay 1d. then some individual, would agree to pay it for them.

Stapner says that no association could be informed to circulate R.Fs, views on defensive war, because the opinion was not adopted, that it was inconsistent with the Gospel; the propagation of opinions inconsistent with the principles of religion, or of principles not acknowledged would only be their self contradiction; the want of association seems to stop the circulation of all good; the law does not allow more than nineteen persons to collect in one room without giving information to the King, who then immediately orders a military guard to be mounted at the door; indeed, military appear to be placed at every entrance to the public gardens, and scattered all over them, as well as in every street-that the present reign may be said to be one of terror to the subject, than one of love by which Royalty is supported the profligate licentiousness of the old King is spoken of with contempt and detestation by some. Wishing to give his mistress a bible he obtained one with plates, and displacing the lawn paper by which each was protected, he replaced the same with a £1000 pound note before each, and having built her a house he sent the large gold key of it set with diamonds.

7th day

Called on Kiefer, professor of Oriental Languages and translator to the government our discourse turned on the Turkish bible, which he is now in hand with for the Society; he spoke with much calmness on Henderson's and Patterson's opposition had not heard that the Professor of Oriental languages at Cambridge had defended him against Henderson's remarks he had rendered the new Testament into Turkish and showed us some proof sheets of the old as far as Kings.

En passant, I gave one of the Yearly Meeting addresses of last year to an elderly friend of his; it was accepted civilly, he appeared to know something of Friends and their exertions, and asked our address. Sir S.Smith was engaged, Baron Girardo also. Visited Jas. Violette from Bordeaux, by which it appears that the trade is not carried on at Bordeaux except some very trivial shoring, said he was in the trade in his youth on the coast of Africa, had seen in numerous instances slaves placed in formations exactly the same as the pounds of England, miserably dying of diseases or sores, and so effected with insects that no inconsiderable part of the frame was wasted.

7th day

Afternoon at the Gobelins and exceedingly struck with the beauty of the tapestry, exceeded anything I could have conceived possible to be done by the loom. The patterns are taken from the most beautiful paintings, which it appeared to me must be executed in oil colours on canvas to the same shades and size as is intended to be executed on the loom; the mode of warp as conducted in the first room appeared to me to be something of the same principle as that of the imitation India shawls, that surface of the manufacture only being obvious which is covered with all the loose ends of the silk *(of which a small quantity is used in carrying out shades)*, and worsted etc., which on the completion of the work must be cut off-in the next room the weaving was of an entirely different description the basis or warp of cotton was perpendicular from the top of the room to about three feet from the bottom, the thread being arranged as in a common loom; the workman was placed behind the screen of thread or cotton warp and having a strong light before him, he might be said to thread the worsted across the perpendicular warp with the fingers.

The pattern appeared in some degree drawn on the warp as we see it in canvas or rug work the number of pieces suspended from the wall for exhibition were not numerous the work is not carried regularly on like common weaving, but whilst one part of the figure is proceeded with and finished to some extent, other parts of it are not commenced with.

Children generally are sent out to nurse by those who can afford it, soon after they are born, and remain out until fit for boarding school; they remain there until about fourteen, and if females, are very often affianced at that age, and soon married without affection, so that after life becomes a source of violation of all mutual engagement to both parties.

2nd day morning. Called at the Hotel du Ministre found him engaged-in the Salon met with an ecclesiastic and the Bishop of Quimper to whom as two strangers C. and J.F. introduced us, and requested each of their acceptance of a tract on the treatment of Negroes; at the presentment they appeared to shrink from the acceptance, but took them hesitatingly, yet with acknowledgment.

The Parisians having no coal, use charcoal in all their cooking; in all passages or lobbies you see a square stove made of enamelled earthenware, mostly white, having the appearance of common white china. The stove also has a china chimney which at the top of the room is inserted into a general chimney the stove is warmed with charcoal only and will answer the purpose of cooking the fixed (fire) places in the rooms are always without grates, bars or stoves, small faggots of wood or sticks are laid upon the hearth or upon two cross pieces of iron raised two or three inches to keep them from laying close to the hearth and to admit a little air.

Every family appears to roast its own coffee, and this very often conducted in the street; the domestic sits at the door with a small tin cylinder fixed over a chafing dish containing charcoal, and continues to turn the cylinder till roasting is effected. The use of charcoal and wood contributes very extensively to the beauty of the scenery in the squares and public gardens in what may be termed the centre of the city. The numerous and very large scale statues which adorn the gardens and walks retain so much beauty of colour. Nothing but the ideas of the French could tolerate these statues.

4th day

Silent meeting; afternoon, called on Keifer with cousin Fowler Rachael Fowler, of Melsham), thought his wife a very interesting woman, and continued to think very favorably of him. He let us see the congratulatory letter of the Sultan of Constantinople to Louis on his ascending the throne; the document was on paper glazed and stiffened so as to bear an exact resemblance to vellum, the signature was like one ornamented letter done in gold. The evening attended a soiree at Stapner's, many young females and about the same number of men. Frank sociability seemed wanting, and the only way they appeared to have in these parties was a recourse to cards which on the introduction of, we took leave. We received a note this evening from Villele, the Minister of Finance and Secretary of State, fixing an audience with us for the second day next, and from the Duc de Montmorency, Minister of Colonies, fixing an audience for tomorrow. Addressed a note to the Minister of Justice, Cte de Peyronnett, requesting an interview. Notwithstanding our efforts produced but little and seem discouraging we continue to think it the best to claim increased attention to the suffering of the Negroes.

There is an accommodation and selection in Parisian hotels much exceeding anything I have found in England the entrance door from the staircase is into the hall for servants to wait in, and fitted with tables and chairs for daily accommodation; next a handsome sitting room and the lodging rooms in the same line for the same floor; the windows of the hotel generally look into open courts mostly filled with trees, acacias, etc., now beautiful white with flowers; ranged in square green boxes by the sides of the walls in the court are continued rows of Chinese Arbor vitae, which have a pleasing effect and foreign appearance. Here follows notes of calls paid on Le Comte Corbierre, Le Vte. De Castelbajere, and others.

5th day noon.

During our tarrience in the Hall of the Minister of Colonies, surrounded by a number of naval officers in their most superbly embroidered uniforms, who, like ourselves, were waiting for audience and instructions, we introduced respectfully to them the object of our application to the Minister of the Marine, and had a courteous and patient hearing. He received us, very attentively reading a paper we had penned, being the outline of our object. Count Severin Tonnere has a pleasant and interesting countenance. He made some remarks on what our note stated as to the present extent of the outfit of vessels for the slave trade from Nantes and doubted our correctness: to the truth of this we were able to reply. We were able to acknowledge the iniquity of a trade in humane beings and the distress it must involve parents and children, husbands and wives in; he said he had strengthened the forces on the coast of Senegal, and that he just had a captain with him who complained of the seizure and forfeiture of his ship, though he had no slaves on board.

7th day, 6.20

Went to Minister of Finance Villele; he was very polite and skimmed over our paper, and endeavoured to show it would not do for them to make slave carrying a capital punishment, that it would exasperate the traders, lead them to greater acts of cruelty, and that neither judges nor jury would convict. He alleged that they were more vigilant, suppressing as they can and confiscating property, and that if our country would exchange the Isle of France for Goree and Senegal, our Government could then do more as it liked with the coast of Africa. In reply it was said that we did not plead for death as a punishment, but that it should be made criminal, and alluded to many vessels fitted out at Nantes; he said that their officers were on the alert, and when any proofs of the object of the voyage were discovered, the cases were followed up; it was remarked that they should have an increased station on the African coast, he said the trade was less than it had been, and that more care was taken; allusion was made more particularly in the Guinea coast. He was urged to consider the thousands annually enslaved, the miseries and the sufferings sustained, and the disgrace to the Christian name.

We gave him a copy of statements in French. Went afterwards to the Ambassador, he was not so courteous; did not trouble him long, thinks he can do little. The American Minister was working with more effect. The British Consul at Nantes is deeply interested in suppressing the trade and has been over to our Government to state facts; he said that there had been several vessels on the Eastern coast of Africa which he had represented to the Government. Evening at Versailles, tea with S. Lloyd, who accompanied us to the Petit Trainon, the favourite residence of the famous Josephine, consort to Bonaparte. I consider this in its simplicity and beauty as excelling anything I have seen in France, the style of English and some parts resembles Studley. One part is very interesting called the Swiss Farm-the dairy, the cow house, the mill, the maison du Cure, the cottage and every part remarkably Swiss.

The Palace of Trainon is a small, compact place of little or no magnificence, but the scenery is enchanting the front commands a fine view of the Palace of Versailles, with which it communicates along some avenues the back is divested of all the cut tree formalism of Versailles, and which generally attaches to the grounds of Trainon, but I have seen no trees in the country which I should call fine trees, nothing comparable to our venerable oaks and elms in England. This part of the Palace of Versailles which fronts the town has a fallen, neglected state, and the whole appearance of Versailles, which once contained 90,000 inhabitants and now 27,000, has rather a desolated aspect. The Palace which fronts into the grounds, is magnificent beyond any building I have seen, and the view from the terrace into the grounds commands the opening of several avenues in each of which are either immense marble basins with Tritons and other figures or remarkable fountains. The quantity of polished Italian marble in steps, basins, and statues innumerable exceeds anything I could of conceived. The Orangery is very extensive and to an English eye must be exceedingly striking; there are several hundred, and just about breaking into flowers; perhaps few scenes in the world are calculated to furnish the contemplative mind with a field so expansive as this, where human grandeur is the subject of musings what a lesson to the proudest and most elevated in life is here presented: the residence of that proud monarch Louis X1V., and the scene of his intimacy and finally of his marriage with Madam Maintenon.

2nd day afternoon

Seated under the cedars of Lebanon in the Jardin des Plantes, surrounded by very interesting objects; this garden is very extensive and may be said to commemorate Bonaparte's greatness of mind. Although it did not owe its origin to him yet his genius enriched it with specimens of natural history, the elephant, the elk, and numerous animals walking about in their own enclosures neatly and rustically divided. The more tame animals were numerous: goats, verities of deer, sheep, etc; the collection of birds not numerous; a great variety of eagles most striking.

Year 1838

Sun, Feb 25.

Proposed to Abigail Thorpe to accept the position of housekeeper, to me after my dear daughter Rachel leaves me, to have £40 per annum, to take the general over sight of my indoors establishment, the care and spread of my table except in my dear daughter's presence.
(Rachel his daughter was engaged and married in August 1838, to Richard Fry of Bristol. She died in 1853, and her husband in 1878)

Mar 1. Hired Joseph Gatenby to come (as a man servant) at £20 per annum, to have two new suits, two hats and one morning jacket each year, and an upper coat once in two years.

Tues. Mar 6th The last remains of snow, which has fallen at intervals ever since the 2nd of 1st. mo., and in rather uncommon quantity, disappeared today.
April 3rd our Quarterly Meeting. We had a large share of the Company of our friends, about thirty dined with us.

April 30 This day the intelligence reached me of the birth of a son, to my dear son, and daughter, Henry and Anna, at Middleton St. George.

Mon., May 7th - Dined at Jonathan Pims, sailed for Liverpool in the evening. On the passage ruminated on a very disturbed close of the yearly meeting yesterday from a friend kneeling and commencing an extended supplication after the meeting had risen.

[Yearly meeting in Dublin]

Tues. May. 8th – Reaching Liverpool this evening after a remarkably fine passage (twenty four hours), and proceeded on our way towards Walden by the Grand Junction Railway to Birmingham, thence to Lamington. . .

Attends the yearly meeting in London and returns for a fortnight or so to Saffron Walden.

Mon., June 18 – Left my dear son and daughter Gibson...This dearly loved pair, blessed with the blessings of the heavens above and of the earth beneath-very ardent are my longings that they would bring their tithes unto the storehouse of their bounteous Lord. . .

Thurs., June 21 – (Darlington). The access to our Meeting-house is at present incommoded by moving a range of cottages, a stable and the small Meeting-house next the street.

Fri. June 22 – Gave notice to Gervas Robinson, the Registrar, of daughter Rachel's proposed marriage, when he took her signature. My affection for this precious daughter, my lonesomeness when she is gone are pervading feelings of my mind and they may be the sole causes of this mysterious reluctance which I have in resigning her to the Friend who, I believe is sincerely attached to her.

Tues. June 26 – At St. Helens. Called this evening on a few poor friends – on one of them to considerable satisfaction-pilgrims who desire to be on their way to heaven do well to communicate with each other about the road. Visited that which to me is a hallowed spot (i/e his wife's grave)

Thurs. June 28th – Almost universal idleness, feasting and rejoicing on this day of the Coronation of Queen Victoria.

. . . Oh, for a more Christian way of celebrating what are deemed auspicious events. . . A confused company to feast at the opening of John Fell's Mill to end up as it begins.

Fri. June 29th – Some mournful feelings are mine on learning that some of our young men are among the festive parties of yesterday; scenes of music and clamorous noise ought to be held in great repugnance by all sober Christians.

Wed. July 4th – Low and tried during the whole of this day. Returning from (Sunderland) from the Quarterly Meeting in the carriage with Edward and Rachel, I was silent nearly the whole of the way, nothing could raise or cheer me, the contemplation of having so soon to part with my beloved daughter to Bristol, etc., absorbed me. Richard Fry came in the evening.

Fri. July 6th Received a summons to attend the grand

jury on the 23rd inst. After pondering my conscientious difficulties therein, I attended, and thinking it might be in my power to be excused, I was best satisfied to acquiesce and maintain a care not to put questions after the oath was administered. The ground of my willingness now to attend is founded on my wish to find an opportunity for pressing on the jurors, the propriety of using some efforts towards substituting declarations instead of oaths. The advance of Christian principles, however little may be gained at once, is worthy of an effort.

Sat. July 7th Admonished a Friend who I feared was backsliding; his worthy father a humble minister in our Society. The love of company and ardent love of tobacco, and some love of liquor, to some minds seems sure captivity. On my way sifted my motives to what impelled me to this task, found my station as an overseer demanded it, my love and gratitude to my lord called for the service, but perhaps stronger than this was the sense that should this Friend lose his inheritance in heaven. . .

Sun. July 8th Attended a Public Meeting at Stockton this evening, appointed by my dear son (John Pease); it was not large, the peace-bestowing influence of the government of Christ on individuals and kingdoms was set forth; the auditory was settled and attentive, and the meeting ended solemnly after a supplication from John and cousin M. Atkinson.

Sat. July 14th Yesterday my dear Edward had one of his trying attacks; how tenderly I feel for this beloved son in this afflicting permission of divine goodness, but what a favour that no murmur repining or complaint escapes his lips though cut from many of the occupations and enjoyments which vigorous health and the bloom of life is fraught with.

Fri. July 20th A few days of mournful desertion: heavens as brass. Some remembrance of the patience of the cripple by the side of Bethesda who after a patient wait by the side of the pool for thirty eight years, was healed by the Lord – Lord remember me.

Mon. July 23rd At Durham on the Grand Jury, endeavoured with Liddel, the Chairman and some of the Jurors, to obtain their favourable consideration of adopting declarations instead of Oath's agreeable to a bill of Lord Denman's, just rejected. Herein I made in conjunction with my cousin Edward Backhouse, but little way. Returned home same evening after viewing the prisoners and the interior of the

Jail. In point of order, cleanliness and accommodation vastly superior to those dungeons in which ancient Friends suffered.

Mon. Aug. 13th He records 'Rachel's property which she takes to Richard Fry at the time of her marriage', The total is £4,670 and includes '10 Railway Shares S. & D. £2,500; 10 half Railway Shares (125) £1,250,' etc.

Thurs. Aug.16th My beloved daughter Rachel married this day to Richard Fry. . . . We had a sorrowing parting, whether ever to meet again or under what circumstances is veiled from me.
Tues. Aug. 21 Attended the monthly meeting at Cotherstone. . .There was two presentations of marriage, viz.: Henry Broadhead, of Leeds, with cousin Eliza. Backhouse; and John Harris with Mary Ann Mason, of Penrith. After the meeting went to Middleton in Teesdale.

Sat. Aug 25th Went to Newcastle. The Town very busy on account of the Scientific Meetings which have been held there during the past weekend which concluded this evening. The advancement of science and general knowledge is the ostensible object, but hundreds of the most respectable inhabitants of various kingdoms assemble for curiosity, display and amusement. To such it is an idle lounge and waste of time, etc.

Fri. Aug 31st Reading Henry Martin's life and letters I am forcibly struck with his piety, his zeal, the renunciation of self-consideration that he might serve the lord Christ. What am I? How do I spend this evening of my life?

Sun. Sept. 2nd At Croft this afternoon with my devoted and industrious cousin, H.C. Backhouse, at a public meeting.

Wed. Sept. 5th My nephew and niece, Joseph and Jane Clay came.
On Monday, September 10th He accompanied his son John, to pay ' A little debt of Gospel love laid upon him to assemble the inhabitants of Guisborough', Whitby, and Ayton', 'The meeting at Guisborough was large, satisfactorily held.' On the Tuesday they travelled over the moors to Whitby where all the remarks respecting the meeting at Guisborough fully apply'. . . 'We were kindly and hospitably accommodated by Jos Sanders and his wife'. The next day they held a public meeting at Ayton, but here there was not 'that openness to receive the Gospel message.' They remain at Langbarf' (the Richardson's).

Thurs. Oct. 18th Five years have this day run their course since the departure of my inestimable and most unspeakably dear Rachel. . .

How vivid, how fresh the solemnity of that day and that hour when I clasped her dying hand till the pulse ceased to beat.

Fri. Oct. 19th Five years have now passed over me as a widower; the present time compared with the past oftentimes feels lonesome and dreary.

Sat. Oct. 20th At Newcastle attending to a manufacturing concern I have an interest in there. In the evening found that my mind had been too much occupied in consideration of its prospects and gains.

Mon. Oct. 22nd Returned home from Newcastle, where I learnt that my cousin Samuel Lloyd had been baptised with water, and I deplored it. What a delusion of the adversary I believe this to be – believing, as I do, that if I am baptised into the spirit of my Lord and Saviour, Jesus Christ, it is that cleansing and purifying baptism which sanctifies the soul and fits it for an entrance where all is peace and joy.

Mon Oct29th At Middlesbrough, where a large concourse was assembled to see the Duke of Sussex who was this day invited to a public breakfast. I had no share in this festivity. I had some care of four of my grandchildren, but with my views of the retiredness of Christian life, etc., the evening had no sweet peace as the reward of a well spent day.

Sat. Nov. 3rd Anxious to leave all things in good order, I considered my Will and directed it to be re-drawn; very solicitous that it might form the very nearly equal distribution and be to the satisfaction of all my beloved children. If in the residue there is little extra to dear John and Joseph from their having long unprofitably toiled in the business in which) I placed them, but having since tended to advance my property it is my wish.

Sun. Nov. 18th Endeavoured tenderly to reprove a backslider for neglect of meeting, and other inconsistencies. He had not been out to meeting, it was near seven o' clock, his dinner, wine and tumblers and music books were on his table warned him my entreaty was that of a Father counselling, warning and expostulating with a son.

Wed. Nov. 28th James Pike came for his sister Lydia, an open, ingenuous young man engaged in an exposed position in a Steam packet office in Liverpool.

Mon. Dec. 3rd Lydia Pike, after a two months residence, left me accompanied by her brother James. My heart yearns for the preservation of this amiable young woman of eighteen, her lot seems cast in a slippery place. (Pikes were old Irish Quaker stock)

Wed. Dec. 5th In a sense of the remarkable mercy and loving kindness of my God, I have this day concluded it right to set apart small sums to be distributed by my executors after my decease, to poor friends and for other useful purposes, but besides all the temporal blessings and gifts so liberally bestowed, my spirit yet more reverently returns thanks for that grace and truth which came by Jesus Christ, my hope of redemption.

Thurs. Dec. 13th Executing my will this day produces some solemn reflections that when it comes into force my humble hopes is my spirit may, through the revelation and merciful mediation of my intercessor and Redeemer, be at rest in His eternal kingdom-joining the spirit of my beloved.

Fri. Dec. 14th My dear son Edward poorly the thought of being bereft of his affectionate and sweetly innocent and to me endearing society depresses my poor mind, which deeply and keenly feels how bereaved I am-comparatively lonesome my home feels since my beloved daughter left me.

Mon. Dec. 17th Discouraged and effected in seeing the languid and reduced state of my precious son, Edward, and the suffering he so meekly endures. . . . .

Tues.Dec.18th Not much difference in the situation of my beloved Edward; my tenderest feelings and my deepest sympathy is excited. May it stand consistent with the will of the Holy and righteous Judge to restore to me this only and last dear remains of my large family as my indwelling companion.

Wed. Dec. 19th Dear Edward still ill and after a painful and very wearisome tossing night, whilst in much tender feeling for him I inquired if he was favoured with a quite mind; turning his face to the wall he remained silent a while, and whilst a tear appeared to flow over his cheek, replied 'I do'.

Sat. Dec. 29th On considering my practice for several past years of never retiring to my bed until I have read one or two chapters of the Holy Scriptures, and the like care every morning ere I leave my chamber, I feel I have to lament the evanescent abiding of the sacred truths I read, yet I cannot give up the practice as the desire of my spirit is sometimes granted that portions may, during the day, arise for my comfort and instruction.

The year ends with his son Edward a little improved.

Year 1839

January 5th How incorrect is the opinion that a state of perfection cannot be arrived at; he condemns the words of our blessed Lord 'Be ye perfect' as useless, and it denies his ability to make his creatures perfect, and impeaches His willingness to effect it. Surely the Captain of Salvation has both the will and the power to perfect his soldiers
Sat. Jan. 19th My grandson, Joseph Whitwell Pease, went yesterday to John Ford's Boarding School at York.
Mon. Feb. 11th Paid Abigail Thorp her first half year's wage of £20.

Tues. Feb.19th My property being apparently on the increase, and already far exceeding all that ever I could ask or think, my earnest desire is that I may become less attached to it, and more and more anxious to be ready to distribute in poor channels, ever ready to listen and obey the pointing of the finger of the adorable donor.

Thurs. Feb. 28th Attended the weekday meeting, it was encouraging to see friends so well out to me it was a low season-can these dry bones live? My beloved daughter Emma this day confined of her ninth child, a son.

Sat. Mar. 2nd Went home at noon; had seven of my dear Joseph's children and himself to dine. I looked round with gratitude in the enjoyment of having them dear Henry, who had returned from Belmont the day before, and Richard Fry were of the company.
Edward constantly had someone to dine with, mostly family, traditional Quaker dress was worn. The dinner hour was 2.30, Edward kept an exceptional table, Silver linen, china, glass, tankards were all the best,. Beer was always provided and after the cloth was drawn, heavy cut-glass decanters of port, Lisbon, Madeira, and Buccellas wines were placed on the mahogany with dessert. The fruit from his garden and greenhouse Was famous, especially his plums, apricots, and apples. The cultivation of which Edward took great delight and interest.

Mon. Mar. 4th Became dry and empty and poor by spending too much time ought I to spend any?) in reading narratives, travels, anecdotes and news. Endeavoured in the evening to turn inward, a little sweetness was afforded, in meditating on the attributes of the Most High as the Author of Mercy, the God of Love, and the God of the Spirits of all the Flesh. And, oh, awakening and solemn thought, the god to whom all flesh must come and who judgeth according to every man's work.

Tues.Mar.5th Solicited yesterday to subscribe £500 in unison with many Friends for the purchase of land in Jamaica whereon to locate the Negro population now free. I declined to subscribe, my observation and experience affording me no encouragement to trust that peace, harmony, and utility would be likely to follow this joint stock trading in a satisfactory way. The comfort of the Negroes and some profit were contemplated I hope some of the former will result profit from sales to Negroes!

Tues Mar.19th My dear Edward's languid looks effect me. He walked down as far as the hot-house, found the ascent back rather trying. Advised a dear Stockton Friend to take no share or interest in a new bottle house to be erected.

Thurs. April 4th Anxious and depressed. Another surgical operation being deemed needful in my dear Edward's case, Dr. Baird of Newcastle came to perform it. His view of the case is on the whole discouraging, the pain was born with exemplary patience; this case and my dear daughter Anne (his son Henry's wife) are sources of deep anxiety. Was informed of the very sudden decease of Barbara Palmer who appeared well at meeting this forenoon a peaceful friend, a quiet spirited widow.

Fri. April 5th The increase of my stewardship by the remittance of £1000 from the Forth Street concern (Stephenson's Engineering Works, Newcastle) should tend to rivet on me forcibly the necessity of enlarged benevolence; may an eye to see a heart willing to distribute be given me as my gracious Lord commits more to my charge.

Wed. April 10th A remarkable sweet covering was over many of our spirits as we stood round the grave of Barbara Palmer. In reverence I accepted it as an evidence that she was entered in the rest of her Savior, who she often said was her only hope. This pious female was laid very near where my greatest earthly blessing lays reposed; how often have my feet visited that spot and my spirit been refreshed there

Mon. April 29th Accompanied a few friends, who had received summonses to pay Church rates, in their attendance on the magistrates, and used some endeavours to prove that the words all chapels included those of deserters and that notices of the rate according to the words of the act were required to be placed on the doors of such chapels; this was overruled, as well as other reasons advanced,

five justices being present.
In May he attends the yearly meeting in London, in the company of Mary Leckies and J. Hadwenas as far as Belmont. On

Monday 20th May, he attends a meeting of Elders and Ministers, and says that the 'afternoon was much occupied in considering propriety of sending down a minute of Counsel, chiefly on the subject of plainness of speech. The following day he again attends, when certificates are granted to E. Robson, and Daniel Wheeler to visit America were read; also that for Elizabeth Fry to visit France. In June he is much in his son's sick room, on June 4th Doctor Wishart informed dear Edward he could give but very little hope of his recovery.

The beloved invalid then with great calmness remarked he had for sometime had similar apprehensions, and added "then it is only elevations that are in thy power", . . .When the Doctor informed us of this conversation, it covered the minds of my dear sons and daughters and my own with so great sadness that it appeared to seal expression for some time.
On June 5th 'The information of last evening had such an impression on him that, inquiring for his pocket book, etc., in the morning, he calmly introduced the state of his affairs to dear John's notice, explaining everything that he thought needed to be adverted to. On my being alone with him he expressed his tender love and affection for me, and there was none so suitable to confer with as to the settlement of his affairs. I took down his wishes and the notes were given to the attorney. In the evening, with tears and much tenderness, he expressed his love for his brother John, who was with him, and his desire that the best and richest of blessings might be showered down on him and his precious family'.

Fri. June 7th Not quite so low a day as yesterday, being able to enter into conversation, desired a fair copy of his will might be read over to him, which being quite agreeable to him he signed it. he was very affectionate and endearing to me in the course of the afternoon; placing his arm round my neck and pressing me to him, he remarked what a poor companion he had been to me and how unable he always felt to make due return for my love and affectionate care of him, that possibly we might not for so long be separated but go to join his precious mother that we might be all united again. I reverently thank my Lord for the sweet and peaceful overshadowing which generally prevailed in the sick chamber of this beloved son.

Wed.June12th My precious

son still continues. At times he entered into sweet, interesting converse; his mind is centered in peaceful trust in the mercy of his Redeemer, and in his chamber there is that witnessed which feels as a confirmation that a prepared spirit is ere long to ascend to him who gave it. My heart in all its tenderness of feeling is enabled to give thanks for that life and immortality which is granted by the coming and offering of our Blessed Lord.

Mon. June, 17th This day in his thirty ninth year my beloved Edward's earthly probation sweetly, peacefully closed. His life might be said to be one of unspotted innocence and integrity: uprightness and a tender conscience were conspicuous in all his conduct, in all his transactions he was remarkable in his care to put the most charitable construction on the words and doings of all: his watchfulness and piety were exemplary; he was dearly beloved by us all, for he was worthy. . .

Tues. June17th Thankful for the feeling granted me in sitting by the remains of my dear son. My spirit forcibly was impressed with a sense of Blessedness of them that die in the Lord the fluctuations of life, its cares, its toils, its temptations and its intricacies are forever exchanged for a glorious rest! What is there worthy of pursuit compared with such blessedness.

On the 21st he sits by the coffin some time, and records his feelings.

On the 22nd He receives his 'Aunt Bragg and cousins J.&R. Priestman,' and rejoices to have 'all my dear sons and daughters with me (except dear Anna). Henry came, leaving his Anna very languid and reduced at Tunbridge Wells.'

Sun. June 23rd A solemn day for me. The interment of my dearly beloved, my tenderly affectionate son. A very large attendance of the inhabitants of this place and Friends from Stockton proved the estimation in which his virtuous Character was held. As his unoffending life had been one of great quietude and peace, so in dying and at the end all was peace, in a large and solemn meeting. One removal more and then my house will be desolate of all its family occupants.

Tues. July 9th Much engaged with my hay in troublesome wet weather. Much unsettlement and rioting in Birmingham, excited by those called Chartists, who want a Charter of equal rights and suffrages in Parliament, etc. Unsettlements has been no uncommon occurrences amongst the inhabitants of this favoured Isle and from it some of our best and most tolerant principles and privileges have sprung. Though unpleasant and sometimes attended with distressing circumstances, I neither fear their operations nor dread their ultimate effects; to such I think we must look for an improvement in the Ecclesiastical state.

Wed. July 10th Joseph (his son, M.P. for South Durham) arrived at home from attending Parliament. The efforts of the Liberal members are rendered so abortive by the power of the Tories in the House of Peers that hardly any service is more discouraging than the spending of time in endeavouring to frame good laws, conscious at the time they will not be suffered to pass. May it please Omnipotence so to overrule the counsels of men that all they do may have a tendency to introduce harmony, happiness and righteousness into the kingdoms of men.

Fri. July 26th Finished again the notes needful for the republishing of my will.

Sun. July 28th Received the account of the decease of my beloved daughter-in-law, Anna, who died at St. Leonard's on the morning of the sixth day last, being the 26th inst. Very sweet is the remembrance of this amiable minded daughter her end was peaceful, her resignation and patience in a long, wasting illness proved a fine disposition and well regulated mind. My dear son, after a very endearing union of four years, becomes a widower at the age of thirty-two with only one son.

Mon. July 29th At St. Helen's Auckland an accident by fire damp having accord in the Coal Mine there, in which I was interested, and seven (men & boys) being so severely burnt that four have since died, it was my Concern that by calling in additional medical aid and every means the remaining three might be most kindly taken care of, it was a satisfaction to learn they were in a fair away to recovery, and sundry adaptations to render the mine safe was directed to be immediately carried into effect.

Tuesday, 30th July, he leaves home to attend the funeral of Mrs. Henry Pease, his daughter-in-law, at Uxbridge, and on his way calls at Doncaster 'on my worthy ancient friend, Richard Cockin and his wife.' The following day, still travelling he records, 'I have never seen the Country, at least as far as Grantham, more inundated, or the crops. . . more pressed down and laid flat. This is a critical period-exceedingly small is the supply of grain left in the Kingdom,' On Friday, 2nd August, he attends the funeral of his daughter- in-law, and soliloquizes on the passing of beauty and the vicissitudes of life and quotes-

'So flourishes and fades majestic man,

Fair is the bud his vernal morn brings forth
And fostering gales the nursling fan.'

Tues.Aug.6th Travelling homeward in the mail, in company devoid of much interest, except that of my downcast son.
The next day he arrives home and' found cousin T. Richardson here and also my dear son Joseph; they had been caring about earthly things.'

10th August with his son John sets out to visit Friends in various places where John preaches and where Edward records re-marks of attendance's and completes rough sketches of people who were present, if fully published it would be a very good guide to the strength of the Society at that time, the following are a few of the major Towns and Villages. . . Stockton, Norton, Bishop Auckland, Greta Bridge, Cotherstone, Darley, Rawdon, Barnsley, (lodged at Jervas Brady's, most hospitably entertained), Sheffield, Chesterfield, Mansfield, Nottingham, Castle Donington, (lodged at Bakewell Ellis's), Leicester, (lodged at widow Burgess, dined at Thomas Burgess, Wigstone Grange), Northampton, (lodged at Wm. Collins'), Olney, (only one Friend, Shepherd Bell, (lodged there, was interested here in going into the Summer House, a poor mean place, where Couper wrote his poem, 'The Task'), Newport, Pagnall, Buckingham, Banbury, (lodged at Jos. A. Gillets),Adderbury, Sibford, Chipping Norton, Burford, Witney, Farringdon (lodged at Jane Reynolds), Charlbury, (at Nicholas Albright's, who expresses a few words in meeting. I apprehend his borders in that way may be enlarged'), Newbury, ("Jno. Albright and Samuel Beezeley with us, lodged at Samuel Whiting's ", ...Geo. Payne, "A Friend was mayor of the place, I greatly fear to his marring in every sense"), Warborough, (lodged at widow Green's), Maidenhead, and Henley, (lodged at Jno. Fell's), Reading, Thame,("five individuals keep up a meeting after the manner of Friends. . .in very low circumstances, and meet in a poor cottage near Haddenham"), Wycombe, (lodged at Thomas Edmund's, "John Wilkinson has been painfully scattering here"), Amersham, (" our Religious Society here is nearly extinct, where but a few years ago thirteen families resided", accounts for it by death, removal, and the baneful influence of John Wilkinson"*), Chesham, (about six families here), Leighton Buzzard, ("lodged at John Grant's, his wife, the daughter of Mary Brooks, who wrote on Silent Waiting. J.G. is eighty seven years of age"), Aspley, (at W.T. How's), Berkhampstead, (at

Thomas Squire's), Derby, Leeds, and thence home.

* John Wilkinson (an Evangelical who resigned his controversial membership of the Friend's in 1835,).

The lonely old man gets to his house on the 28th September, some remarks made by him at the time of his journey call up passing events such as the Chartists Agitation, or the Oxford Movement.

16th. Oct he completes his will, and then reverts again to his having given more to his sons than daughters, and goes on. . . .
"I would observe they entered on a business that had been beneficial to me, but has never yet rewarded their toil, yet their continuance of it and their great efforts to advance the family interest in various ways have tended through divine permission to be blessed, and remuneration from the common stock is justly due.

Fri. Dec.27th. The accounts from my Irish correspondent of the ranting spirit of two woman travelling amongst them and disturbing their meetings in the north and the state of Friends generally in Ireland afflicts my spirit.
On the last day of the year he reviews his spiritual state, thanks heaven for his own uninterrupted health, remembers the dead, and in temporal matters takes a gloomy prospect of the coming year.

Year 1840

A year which Edward complains that dear Joseph is involving him in too much responsibility.
This was also the year that Edward negotiated premises for the friends at Seaton.

January: Starting in Scotland
Edward Pease leaves Edinburgh on New-Year's Day, and "came to Melrose and had a meeting for the inhabitants in the evening", which was well attended.

Sat. Jan., 2nd Travelled this day from Melrose to Berwick, forty-three miles; the weather was fine, the ride, much by the river Tweed, was beautiful, the cultivation and land good, the farmyards remarkably stocked with Rick's of corn. . . .Whilst at Edinburgh I heard of the very sudden decease of my dear and valued cousin Ann Mounsey, three or four years younger than myself. She was a virtuous kind, hospitable woman in the station of an elder. She died universally beloved by all who knew her.
The next day, Sunday, Mrs. H.C. Backhouse addresses a meeting of 300 at Spittal and of "1000 at Berwick in a large chapel lent by the minister present."

Mon.Jan.11th United with Annie Hutchinson and Mary Cudworth, paid a visit to Ann Eliza Dale on her request to be united in membership with our Society. She is truly pious minded person and being convinced of the principles has through conscientious conviction taken up, to her, a heavy Cross* [the stiffer Darlington Quakers even objecting to her wearing her wedding ring. Mrs. Joseph Pease (grandmother) never wore hers at Darlington – only when she was away from home].

Tues. Jan. 12th The application of Ann. E. Dale was again left for consideration next month.
On the second of February, at the monthly meeting at Stockton, it was concluded to accept pious A. Eliza. Dale into membership. The mind of the meeting, I think, was weightily ascertained and whilst my judgement did accord there with yet my mind was not void of apprehension that in some way or other this dear individual might not be a source of anxiety to us. Edward later went through a number of letters which he had from himself and also his late wife. He wrote that his family would discover human frailty and weakness; yet they will discover that no union more true, more saintly affectionate and one in purpose ever existed than that between their father and mother.

Mon. Feb. 22nd Met a few Friends to coffer on Cousin Thomas Richardson's munificent offer of £5000 towards establishing an Agricultural School for the children whose parents have been members of the Society. It is comparatively seldom that he takes much notice of anything like business in these diaries. On march 22nd, after spending part of a day at St. Helen's Colliery, he says. . . I am prepared or nearly so to resign my cares[and they have been very small] in this concern to others, the pulling off of harness. . . more and more becomes me, so that when the call comes "all things are ready for thy entrance," no garments may be found on me unfitting for the presence of my Lord.

Sat. Mar. 27th Whilst at Shields yesterday afternoon Isaac Richardson died. He was the son of Henry Richardson of Stockton, before that of Whitby. Isaac Richardson's wife, now widow, was daughter of Joseph Unthank; the deceased died in humble hope of the mercy of his Savior; his had been a life of vicissitude, some trial and some changes[having been a brewer] for conscience sake. It had been much in my observation that whilst Friends may not during life have evinced all that watchfulness or regard for things of a heavenly nature, yet there having been kept up a more than usual care not to offend the Most

High by violating his moral law, though strong confidence is not granted, there is among them a more general humble peace, yielding hope in the end.

Tues. Mar. 30th A day of great bustle and unsettlement from the opening of the Great North of England Railway. Twenty years ago these projects, or rather that from this coal district, was of much interest to my mind and its completion in 1825 may be said to have given birth to all others in this world. For the cause of humanity, at least, I believe them to be useful and being in the permission of infinite wisdom hope they may not be wrong, but I desire to acknowledge with thankfulness that my mind is broken off or weaned from all new schemes.

This year he speaks of the anxieties laid heavily on his shoulders of his son Joseph, because of him, having the heaviest dealings and responsibilities, and he fears heavy losses will be sustained by him.

Sat. June 5th I am free to record that having made a small purchase of some decoration to place on my lawn I am not free of some reproach and condemnation, believing that religion which I have from my Lord, if I am faithful to it, admits but little of self-pleasing in the purchase and use of things which are merely decorative; besides, there is an example to those around us which if they follow, we feel we have been corrupters. . .

On the 12th June he refers to his property at Seaton and what he has given for the Meeting House there, complaining of dealing's with a magistrate who is based there.

Tues.June29th In passing through the town I observe nearly all the windows in the Town Hall are broken by the riotous inebriates of last night. Oh, the wickedness of contested elections; when will the day come . . . when righteousness shall run down as a mighty stream. . .

Wed. July 7th Returned home thankful that the bustle of yesterday, as the day of nomination for members of Parliament, was quietly over, and that my heart was out of all cares and anxieties into which, little to their profit, some of my friends were drawn. Whilst I believe that the Gospel Spirit may allow us to give a vote for the best principled men who offer, yet there are so many measures in which the man who may be said to represent me can and does unite, that I am not free from some reluctant feelings in giving my vote.

Sat. July 10th Concluding day of election, Bowes and Vane the successful candidates; the termination was as orderly as could be expected. Lord H. Vane lodged at my house, which afforded an opportunity of frank and friendly converse; he appears am amiable man, friendly to religious liberty and non-Ecclesiastical assumption. Went to Middlesbrough with dear Joseph to see the Docks drawing to completion. I should have enjoyed such commercial advantages, but mental pain and sympathy was my portion in a deep sense of the almost overwhelming load my dear son has to carry. . .

Mon. July 12th A vast concourse in the town to witness the two successful candidates being chaired; great intemperance and tumultuous unsettlement. When will men be wise and a better state of things supervene ?

Thurs. July 15th Some sweet instruction as I meditate over the silent grave of my ever to be beloved and never to be forgotten Rachel, who being dead yet seemed to speak and to encourage me as she often did to live a life of piety, to love and to serve my God and his Church, to be aware of the cares of life that they did not dry up the Spirit of God and as she was kind and tender hearted to the poor and to all, so kindness and tenderness might mark my path. Lord help in all this and in all that is well pleasing to thee.

The next day he mentions that this completes 402nd week since his wife died, remarking that she was the best of heaven's gifts to him on this side of eternity, and also complains that dear Joseph has too much to carry through, for any purse or resources.

Mon Oct.18th This day completed the 416th week since that which bereaved me of heaven's best earthly gift, and as in deep darkness of last night I stood by her grave and whilst the loud stormy wind blew heavily on me, my spirit had some sweet sense of the eternal rest . . . and some hope was granted that when this poor frame came to lay like hers, undisturbed by stormy winds or time or cares, our rest might be together in the Lord. Amen

Thurs. Oct. 21st. The marriage of J. J. Gurney and E. P. Kirkbride very agreeable conducted. . .

Sat Oct 23rd. Accompanied Samuel Gurney in a most interesting journey to Ayton by way of Middlesbrough; his wish was to see cousin Thomas Richardson, and our Agricultural School. The whole day appeared to be much enjoyed by him; his converse was truly instructive to me, his generous and charitable deeds united with true Christian principles seems to establish him in my mind as a friend and brother beloved, if I have any right so to attach myself to a prince of a man.

Wed. Nov.10th Yesterday was the birthday of a son of our Queen Victoria, the probable King of these realms oh, unenviable possession sufficiently large and humbled Christian will feel in that stewardship which the Most High has committed to his charge. . .

Mon. Dec. 20th . . .When I contemplated the engagements of my three dear sons during this day, my heart's desire was that they should all be employed as my first born (John) at Oxford Select Quarterly Meeting, but my second (Joseph) was at Newcastle respecting coals; my third (Henry) at Wolsingham respecting railways these latter may be needful and useful engagements, but a too much divided heart ruffles the tide of peace.

Fri. 24th Went to Seaton to pay for the erection, finishing and seating the Meeting-House I have built there for the use of Friends who may go to that place to bathe. As a small part of my substance dedicated for the purposes of worshipping my most merciful and bounteous Benefactor, my heart most cheerfully returns back to his own homage only that which is his own. The popularity of Seaton as a bathing place among Friends was highlighted on notes found in Edward Pease's possession when in the summer of 1841 over seventy Pease family and friends were notably there on the first day of the summer holidays that year.

Year 1842

Wed. Feb. 2nd In certain circles of our Society resident in London there appears to me a degree of excitement endangering the sacrifice of some of our testimonies while paying attention to the King of Prussia now in England . . .

Sat Feb.12th "The present agitation in the Country for the abrogation of the duty on imported grain may be said to be so great as to threaten a revolution. Being earnestly solicited to sign a petition to Parliament as emanating and confined to Friends of this place, I object there to as recognising the Meeting for Sufferings as the representative body of the Society, and proper organ for the representation of the views of our little Church Friends petitioning from their separate congregations might evince dissononsence of opinion, which as a religious community it ought to be our care and duty to avoid.

This week he again

expresses his dislike of Joseph's taking so much interest in Commercial pursuits and "Some public Work", and wishes he could feel "the unworthiness of such claims on his time and the energies of his fine mind, and be enabled to shake them all off."

Tues Mar. 1st General Meeting of the North of England Railway Company, which I did not attend, nor have I for the last ten years attended any such meetings, fearing to have my mind (naturally very propense to such concerns) engrossed in such cares. . .

Mon. Mar. 7th By all I see, and hear, and read, there appears a very increased desire on the part of the Clergy to grasp aggrandise, and place themselves in a dominant position, but as true as ever the words was spoken to the high priest, "God shall smite thee thou whited wall", so I believe it to be in the Counsels of the Highest, He will smite the whited wall of English prelacy and it's subaltern dependents.

Tues Mar 29th Walked through the Tunnel [this is Shildon Tunnel, the first railway tunnel in the world] not passable for wagons. Such extensive operations and new works awaken my curiosity, but they carry no peace, comfort or solace to my mind; they require such a grasp of mind to undertake and complete them and such an application of time and talent to conduct them that I do not dare to judge how far the Christian should be engaged in them.

Enjoyed a turnout with my ten grandchildren to purchase some sweets, how delightful is such infantile innocence. In April he finds his son John has set his mind on visiting "the few friends at Pyrmont, Mindon, and in the South of France," and though he remarks he is in his 76th Year being blessed with health and vigour, he quires whether he ought not to go too.

Mon. June 6th Entered with my three dear sons into a serious consideration . . . as regards the Mill concerns, how far it may be right at once to wind up . . . The distress it would cause to the poor. . . and a loss of £30,000 to £40,000 to the family appear to render it prudent to try another year. Seeing that it is the will of my good Heavenly Father that wealth should so elude our grasp and knowing how alienating great possessions are I cannot mourn or deplore the dispensation.

Thur Aug.4th Parted with home, all its comforts, endearments and blessings, to accompany my dear son John in his visit to Pyrmont, Minden, and the South of France and Guernsey and Jersey. . . Arrived in London. . . and had good accommodation at the Guildhall Coffee House.

Fri Aug.5th Attended the Meeting for sufferings. . .The Address to the Queen which was agreed on by the Yearly Meeting on the subject of war had not been presented and it appeared that her ministers placed obstacles in the way of its being presented. It had ever been the privilege of our religious Society to present its addresses to the Sovereign either in the closet or on the throne. Spent the afternoon in collecting books, obtaining our passports, etc.
August 10th to 13th In Belgium.
August 13th to 10th September- in Prussia and France.
September 12th to the 10th October - in France.
He then, after travelling 2,500 miles, hurries home to attend the interment of "Jonathan Backhouse, who died in his 63rd.year", and adds:
My clear recollection of attending his father's marriage with my Aunt Ann Pease gives me a view of human changes and the flight of time. [in 1774 Edward being 7 years old]
During December this year it seems Henry Pease was considering the question of asking the hand of cousin, J.M.B. in marriage.

Sun. Dec. 25th. Accompanying the remains of a poor but pious man not a member of our Society, Major Shout, to the last earthly abode we (Sophia Pease and myself) were met by dear Joseph with the distressing announcement that his dear brother John (Sophia's husband) had fallen at the Euston station and broken his thigh. Almost oversetting as the deeply afflicting tidings were we concluded to go to the meeting. . .We left that afternoon to be in London early next morning.
This was a very bad accident, a compound comminuted fracture, and nearly cost John his life. Though weights on a pulley on his bedfoot were long attached to the foot in order to prevent the leg from being shorter than the other, this treatment was not quite successful, for, as I can recollect, he walked with a limp to the end of his life.

Year 1843

New entries begin with concern for John's injury, and his steady recovery. The 26th January finds him at Belmont with the Fells (his son Henry's boy, Henry Fell Pease, was then apparently living with his grandparents, Richard and Mary Fell). He speaks of his dear little grandson, Henry Fell Pease, a lovely child, yet something in his sweet countenançe effects me as indicative either of a sickly deceased frame, if life is continued, or the greater probability that divine wisdom may see meet to cut existence seems almost lost in doubt as to the beneficial results—that humanity has been benefited in the diminished use of horses and by the lessened expense in travelling is obtained, but as to the results and effects of all that Railways have led my dear family into, being in any sense beneficial is unchristian.

Thurs.Aug.17th —Went in the forenoon to Tapton House, late G. Stephenson's residence, and received from Robert a welcome reception; had a serious friendly conference with him, under a feeling expressed to him on my belief that it was a kindness to him his father was taken, his habits were approaching to inebriety; his end was one that seemed painfully to feel no ground, almost, for hope. I fear he died an unbeliever—the attendance of his funeral appeared to me to be a right step due to my association with him and his son. I do not feel condemned in doing so, yet gloomy and unconsolatory was the day. In the church I sat a spectacle with my hat on, and not comforted by the funeral service.

George Stephenson was not much of a church attender, but he had many fruits of the spirit, at least, with his simplicity, honesty, patience, industry, and love of his fellowman, and lastly he prided himself in having a great deal of perseverance needed for his many challenges in life.

Sat. Aug.26th —Looking round my pecuniary possessions I see everything except the Fourth Street concern sinking and wearing an air of deep gloom, shrouding the mind with a multitude of fears, so that contemplating a reduction of property only creates anxiety that there may be enough to fulfill all claims on me and my family, honourably as to the truth.

Tues. Aug. 29th. . .Silvanus Fox came in the afternoon. . .In the exercise of his gift there is a frequent brightness, and it appears to have a right evidence, yet its power did not perhaps from the redundancy of words deepen or much edify my spirit

Thurs. Sept. 7th—At Winyard, went with dear Joseph and his three daughters. Our object was to induce the Marquis to enter into some regulations to avert the ruinous consequences of the coal trade. I felt it was late in my life to intermeddle in such matters, the general state of the suffering mining interest and the interest of my family demanded the effort. Our reception was good, but the effort not crowned with success I fear.

Mon. Oct. 9th. Attended my cousin Edmund's bride's visit agreeably, about thirty present. There is this union much to love and admire. My heart longs for their submission to the humbling power of truth. While I fear there is not in my living and in that in which I indulge, that true simplicity; the variety of indulgent viands and the display after tea was beyond what truth would permit me to suffer on such an occasion.

Fri Oct.27th—Cousin Thomas Richardson and Thomas Pease, of Leeds, with me. His (i.e. T. Pease's) piety and humility exemplary; his perceptions of gospel truth are not such has to set him free from some faith in some elementary observance, and his association with what are termed evangelical characters is not unlikely to carry him into the land of bondage and obstruction of the in shining of the Son of Righteousness. Oh, my soul, endeavour to abide in the light without judging.

Early in November Edward was staying at Malton, where he received a good welcome by his hostesses, Ann and Esther Pries where he takes himself to task here for the "affecting heaviness" which" assailed" him in meeting. On the first of December he visits four poor widows in the Almshouses (founded by his mother, Mary Pease), and finds them comfortable, and adds—A little help handed: may I be more alive to the wants of the poor, perhaps not constantly enough the objects of settled or casual relief. He spends an evening to meet Elizabeth P. Gurney, and remarks that the company was a striking "tablet of sorrow and change": All widows and widowers, viz., John C. Backhouse, myself, H.C.Backhouse, Katharine Backhouse, E. Barclay(Mrs. R. Barclay), Eliza P. Gurney and her sister Juliet Clark.

Mon. Dec. 25th—Christmas Day not in any way kept by me—quietly within doors writing letters—quiet mind, I might say almost unhappily so, not having anxiety enough about my Lord . . .

Wed. Dec.27th The accounts of worthy Henry Birkbeck are of a most discouraging character. Great is the doubt of his one being alive; a blow on the skull by the fall of his horse appears to make an irreparable injury, though surgical skill has recently been exercised.

Thurs. Dec.28th Pecuniary I have cause to admire how an effort to serve a worthy youth, Robert, the son of George Stephenson, by a loan of £500, at first without expectation of not much remuneration, has turned to my great advantage. During the course of the year I have received £7000 from the concern of Fourth Street.

On the 29th December, he notes that Joseph and his daughter Jane have gone to "the interment of his (Joseph's) brother H.

Birbeck's remains. May the mourners receive consolation and instruction from the death of this upright character; there is to all a teaching lesson in such solemn events, but yet more strikingly so to the rich. . .The man of extended and prosperous concerns may be taken away in the midst of them. What avails prosperity if it had not been held in godly fear.
The year 1848 ends.

In the following years Arthur Pease notes some changes in his Grandfather's notes as he gets a little older:

Year 1849

This year Edward Pease is very active with Friend tasks, and travels south to Essex, Bristol, London and Manchester, and his diaries are sharp becoming a religious record. He complains of Rheumatism in his knees, which curtailed his walking. This year it is his desire to be useful to his fellow men, this in his 82nd year.

Year1851

Arthur Pease notes that; As age increases, Edward Pease's piety gains in hope, though the same diffidence is always in evidence. In January he is in Walden, where he is surrounded by the care and attention that a daughter's love and those around can bestow: "by day there is abundance of the finest of wheat; by night the softest of downey beds and pillows, always free from want, misery and pain."

Fri. Jan 10th — Walden. The agricultural distress of this district is very great, the low price of grain very much impoverishing farmers, and the general want of employ for the labourers is the cause of much misery to them; 100 persons were taken into the workhouse one day this week—they seem driven to desperation and being without religion subjection, wickedly burn down the premises and stacks of the farmers. It was observed by one, that he had seen such a burning every night last week.

Mon. Jan.20th Much indoors; read some parts of the book of common prayer, as edited and published by good virtuous, fine minded Judge Bayley, for whom I had a strong friendship.
The following day he is anxious as to how his son Joseph's "meeting with a considerable company of disappointed Stockton and Darlington [railway] Shareholders" in London will go off, and expects that he will have to bear "altogether unmerited the brunt of it, for the sacrifice of property, time and talent, and unwavering patient integrity, has ever been given to the interests of that concern," he is "thankful that he has borne all with exemplary

patients and meekness." But the meeting goes off "tolerably agreeably," and he hopes his sons will take the chance of getting "free from all this turmoil," but "fears if Redcar Harbour is made, the cares of my sons will increase, as they will be looked to." He relates the same week that, "every Friend in Walden attends the week day meeting regularly and that this is their very commendable practice both on the first day forenoon's and afternoons."

Wed. Feb.29th—Having read in Thos. Kimber, Jun's letter to my son John, of a striking conversation he,. T. K. had at Lyons with Hughes, the roman catholic [note no capitals] Archbishop of New York, by which it was obviously the design of the Romanists to limit all history and literature to their dark designs, I sent a copy of the converse to the Archbishop of Canterbury with a desire to place him in possession of their views and my wish that the grant to Maynooth school might be discontinued.

On the 1st of February he is once more at home, and is "delighted to meet all my beloved children and grandchildren in the course of the day." On the 7th "however innocent and amusing an evening was spent in a private exhibition by Nephew Joseph Whitwell of his magic lantern, I feel in measure condemned. . . remembering the time is short !"

Discovery of Ironstone at Cleveland

Sat Feb.8th—great are the anticipation's of advantage to the railway and many parties connected to the iron trade from the discovery of rich extensive veins of ironstone under Eston Nab, and continuing to run South in the line of the Cleveland Hills.

Sat.Feb 22nd—My dear granddaughter, E.P. Gibson, came last evening. Great political changes—the Prime Minister, Lord John Russell, resigns. The prosperity of the Kingdom was great, and all seemed settled peace and safety when the plan of abated taxes was brought in by a blundering Chancellor of the exchequer, which not being carried, of course the ministry must be formed anew with or without a dissolution of Parliament.

Mon.Feb. 24th —The vast departure in our religious society from the simplicity of the gospel and the example of Friends in my early days, in language, in furniture, pictures and decorations, is such that should Friends proceed in deviation for another generation as they have done, they will wear out Quakerism.

Sat. Mar1st—Nothing settled as to our Government Legislature, the alliance of all the papist Members for Ireland bids fair for creating a troublesome opposition if any steps are taken to counteract the arrogant pope's bull.

Thurs. Mar. 6th —The marriage of my granddaughter Rachel [to Albert Lithium] this day solemnised was in a large and crowded meeting very still and well behaved; it felt to me a peculiarly solid sweet feeling of peace on our first sitting down. . . .I humbly ventured to hope it was earnest of a union that ere its close would have evident sanctioning evidences of being marked with divine approvance.

Sat.Mar15th—Increased feelings of rapid breathing in walking and in ascending rising ground tell me the powers of existence are rather rapidly diminishing and it may be some accumulating water may be in my chest and, at some nearly approaching day, close suddenly my pilgrimage. . . .

Mon., Mar., 17th —Last year an income five times more than my expenditure, this year not an income equal to its worth. S and D Railway shares once deemed worth £360 have been sold at £30, so that this property, once deemed worth £60,000, now worth £3000.

Sun. Mar 30th —This being the Government appointed day for taking the numbers in dissenters' meetings, the enumeration in ours was in the forenoon 187, in the afternoon 167.

Tues. April.1st — Agreeable to the permission of the yearly meeting, and accorded with our monthly meeting, that grave stones might be placed on the graves, I directed one to be laid

	£
12 mo. Loss on Pease's West	*2,029*
1 mo. do Ditto	*973*
12 mo do Edward Pit	*333*
3 mo do Pease's West	*1,490*
3 mo do Edward Pit	*594*
2 mo do Adelaide	*381*
3 mo do ditto	*457*
1 mo do South Durham	*141*
2 mo do ditto	*79*
3 mo do ditto	*156*
losses	*6,633*
gains	*1,084*

where the remains of her, my precious companion, was laid, and the letters cut,

Rachel Pease
AE 62, 1853
How soon he who faithfully and inexpressibly affectionately fulfilled his sacred, inviolable promise may require
Edward Pease,
AE 185 .
is known only to my Lord, whom I desire to serve and do Love.
The following is the attitude of an elder to a question of "marrying out":

Sat. April 12th —Tomorrow with Is. Sharp to visit ****** who, in being married to a person not a member at a register office has violated our rules, yet by this act he has violated no moral law. Yet great would be that confusion and trouble if such unions were sanctioned by meetings—the way to unsuitable unions would be made easy—neither would it yield] that discretion nor that religious solemnity, and that religious bearing which is safe and desirable, and if there was offspring the responsible care of them would not, probably, be consistent with our profession.

Wed May 7th —My beloved Joseph now busily engaged in London on the Tees Conservancy Bill, and one regarding the financial state of the Stockton and Darlington Railway, also some cases about Redcar Harbour. I regret the load of care. . . he goes to the yearly meeting in London.

Wed. May 21st —A strenuous effort was made by Jos. Sturge, Chas Gilpin, G. Alexander, and others to have an epistle addressed to our American brethren to stir them up and quicken their zeal to address their legislature on the atrocity of the fugitive slave law. The effort was overruled by a calm deliberation of our relative position, how far we could constitutionally interfere with our brethren there; our correspondence being with yearly meetings.
Edward takes a very serious view of the losses of the Family Collieries, and gives a list for certain months of the losses at the various pits . . .

Saturday 31st May, he enters his eighty-fifth year. Little respecting his work at the Yearly Meeting needs to be quoted, but this reference to John Bright may be of interest: One minute advising Friends not to print anything that may be left on the yearly meeting book for consideration was warmly attacked by John Bright in a strain as unpleasant as proving that he was not acquainted with the constitution of the Society he visits the Great Exhibition, and exclaims, "and a most wonderful exhibition it is: no description could extend to its minutiae." He

spends "four or five hours" there, "greatly gratified, yet on laying my head on the pillow, and remembering how the day had been spent, I thought one hour's communing with, and a feeling of my Saviour's confirming, cheering love, was to me of more value than all my eyes beheld"
He then goes to Bristol. On returning home he records the general condition of crops and weather, and his own hay occupies his care.

Sat July 26th —Marske. Observed the Consett Iron Works Co. making a railway from the ironstone belonging to Lord Zetland to the S.&D. Railway. The growing wheat had a beautiful regular appearance, with a yellowish tinge. Three weeks of fine weather might advance it to fitness for the sickle.
He travels home and goes to see a poor Friend, Thomas Harding. About three weeks ago his leg was amputated; since that time his health has been sinking, and now, heavily panting for breath, his close seems near; he was in a pious disposition of mind; his solitude was great to feel his Saviour near, and my trust was that he was near and would be with him when he was permitted to pass through the valley of the shadow of death. His old wickedness besets him at times.

Mon Aug.,11th—Condemned for the time spent in looking over the Illustrated London News, and reading some of its articles. This work is one of the attractive fascinations of the present times.*[The Illustrated London News was at that time the world's only illustrated paper, it was widely read by the Society of Friends] I received from my most worthily beloved sister Whitwell, a welcome as warm as a long unbroken Sisterly love could give . . . we were comforted in each other's presence.
He then visits Yorkshire.

Fri. Sep.12th—What proofs arise that we build too low if we build beneath the skies ! Twelve months ago nothing could exceed the depression of Stockton & Darlington (Railway). Shares sold for £30, once deemed worth £300, and estimated in my schedule three or four years ago at £250. The change reduces my personal property about £35,000. At this I have no repining, I accept it thankfully for my family and . . . .as permitted for the staining of human glory by a reduction of my children and grand children's portions.

Sat., Oct., 18th —This is the day of the interment of Henry Barclays' remains at Winchmore Hill. May the removal of this dear youth and first cousin to my Grandson, J.W.P.*[Henry Barclay & Joseph Whitwell Pease, were bosom friends and companions, in hunting, and shooting and coursing.] have a teaching effect in it which shall induce him with full purpose of heart to seek first the kingdom of God, and largely staining all that has this world's lure in it.

Wed. Nov. 5th—Now that there is prospects of great advantage from the discovery of iron ore in the Cleveland range of hills, I feel a great anxiety that none of my beloved family may be caught in its enticings; they have quite enough of this worlds engagements. . .Whether it succeed or disappoint, its consequences are to be dreaded.

Fri. Nov.7th —This morning I learn with surprise that Edmund Backhouse has sold Polam to William and Robert Thompson. How great, how rapid the change. So recently was the mansion the very gratifying residence of his beloved mother who, with her husband, had great pleasure in building it and enjoyed its great accommodations and extensive grounds—*sic transit gloria mundi!*

Sat. Nov.15th —I see in the paper a Notice for a railway near Guisborough; the prompting cause is the abounding of Ironstone in that vicinity. This prospective scheme introduces my mind into many doubts and fears as to the inviting of my family.

Snow comes early this year, and Edward mentions Joseph and Emma, not being able to get to Castleton on the 18th November, because of the very deep snow and snow drift. Edward's patience is tried when Joseph talks constantly of Coke, coal, ironstone, and the Fourth Street concern, and the Guisborough Railway, and wishes his "mind would seek refuge" elsewhere. In a review of his past life he reflects that he was never anxious to make money, and that he was more concerned in providing necessary provisions for his numerous family.

On Tuesday, 30th he goes to Smelt House to the funeral with his daughter in law, Emma, and records the next day that the year "goes out with much mildness and beauty from the clearness of the atmosphere," and takes a more cheerful survey of his behaviour and progress during it than usual.

The Diary for the year 1852 is missing

Year 1854

Fri. Jan.6th —Very cold frost with extraordinary deep snow in the southern parts of the country. I fear many of the poor in London are perishing for want of coals. The price has recently been 40s. per ton, and some report them as now 60s.

Mon. Jan. 9th The price of grain continues to advance and' tis becoming very serious to the poor. The price is about eleven shillings per bushel. Except for masons and agriculturists, wages are as equal and employment plentiful. A subscription much too small is entered into the soup and coals are provided for the aged and infirm and those of limited parish allowance.

He continues his visits to Friends' families; as usual, he names them and counts the adult individuals he visits; this month his total reaches a hundred.

On Thursday the 19th., he mentions that his son Henry, yielding to the desire of the meeting for sufferings goes along with Robert Charlton and Joseph Sturge, with a memorial to the Emperor of Russia, I suppose imploring him to put a stop to the effusion of blood and human misery now affectingly carried on with the Turks.

Sat Jan. 21st—Seeing that it hath pleased the Lord to place me from my extreme age, my son John from his favoured gift, my son Joseph from having been in Parliament, my son Henry as going to the Emperor of Russia in conspicuous positions, my Soul longs that I and my descendants may be preserved in great humility and watchfulness, that the Lord may condescend to order all our steps and that we dishonour not His name.

Tues. Jan. 24th—At Ayton . . .On arrival at home found a letter from beloved Henry there with A. Mundhenck, at Dusseldorf, expecting to be at Berlin last evening. A gentleman from Warsaw doubts their being allowed to enter Russia. If all fail, hope they may have peace in having done what they could.

Wed Jan 25th—When I consider my sons and daughters, my dear John and his Sophia with their two daughters, my dear Joseph and his Emma, their seven sons and four daughters, my dear Francis and Elizabeth, their son and daughter; my dear Henry and his son, words cannot convey the thankful gratitude I feel. . .The helpers of my infirmities, the strengtheners of my faith, my support, my counsellors and comforters.

Thurs Feb.2nd—This late, this long evening of my life may through divine mercy be said to have a gently descending slope and much of a peaceful quiet thankful mind in the midst of innumerable blessings given me.

Fri. Feb. 19th—Having long been uncomfortable in observing the persons, mostly females, who bring poultry, butter and eggs to market, standing exposed to storms and rain without cover, I have caused one to be attached to the north end of the Town House. It may cost me £100-£130. If it be found to be a protection and add to their comfort, this little appropriation of a part of my blessings is well.

He hears about the safe arrival of Henry at "Petersburg." He is very anxious about his grandson, John Henry Pease, now aged eighteen, who is ill. On the 21st, he mourns the death of "dear and most valuable Wm. Forster," in Tennessee.

Mon., Feb., 20th —Concluded to purchase for schools some premises in Skinnergate for £1,600, expecting Friends will liberally contribute to fit them up for the First-day and other schools.

Wed., Feb., 22nd —Grateful in heart for a good account of my beloved Henry from Petersburg. The object of their visit, through divine favour, has been fulfilled in presenting to the Emperor the address. Their reception was courteous, the resulting effects of it rests with him who rules in the hearts of the children of men. May he bless this endeavour to do what we can to promote peace and good-will.

Fri., Feb., 24th —The public paper The Times*[A cartoon representing Quakers as a braying ass standing in front of the muzzle of a cannon, and articles making fun of their mission and efforts for peace, may be seen in Punch] exceedingly derides and ridicules the Society of Friends for sending the deputation to Russia. So far as yet appears, we have cause for thankfulness; the kindness of its reception by the Emperor has been quite remarkable. His offer to make them presents were declined that no venality might be ascribed to them. His sending one of his messengers to help and haste them on the way was striking . . . . .

Mon., Feb., 27th An interesting evening at East-Mount, the Southend ones present, and we heard with gratified pleasure dear Henry, recite the varied Russian and other Experiences in his travels. . .I planted the new part of the burying ground on three sides with Box and Holly trees. Beautiful weather

Wed., Mar., 1st—The address to the Emperor of Russia with the three Friends presented, now generally appears in the periodicals. It is couched in respectful and beautiful language, expressed with much feeling, and is said to have moved the Emperor to tears of tenderness. I trust the whole matter in every part has been conducted as becomes the Society of Friends

Sat., Mar., 4th The prospects for war increasing and mighty preparations making. Madness and folly, to be rewarded by disappointments; disasters and frustrated counsels, I think will some day be manifest. Tens of thousands of soldiers, sailors and militia to be raised to demoralise this country and impoverish it. May Heaven forbid it All.

Tues Mar 7th Opposition is raised in Parliament against an improved Reform Bill, and parties we had deemed to be Liberal appear against Lord H. Vane, etc. My belief is that from the increasing intelligence of the people various improvements in the legislature and constitution of the Kingdom will take place and an advance in Gospel principles will be more operative and practical.

Wed. Mar15th My Grandson J.W.P. just returned from a visit to his chosen friend. My nephew, John Beaumont Pease, writes me from Stamford Hill a poor sinking account of his uncle, my valued friend William Beaumont . . .

He watches his garden and fruit trees with the same pleasure as of old, and on the 22nd March he notes "the wall begin to look white with apricot and plumb blossom," and other such things. He records this month the journey of his son, John and S., to Allonby, to dismantle my late Cousin Thos. Richardson's dwelling house. A long life sees the desolating of many habitations. . .the kindest hospitality has been experienced under this roof. . .All must now be left desolate and bare. May its owner through mercy rest in blessedness and peace where no change nor any cares can come.

Wed. Mar 29th I hear that war with Russia is declared! very affecting it is to think of the misery that is in store for thousands. . .Surely nations, rulers and legislatures, have much to be accountable for, and neither those in power nor those out of power can form an idea what the calamity will produce or when it will end . . .

Wed. Apr 5th An unsettled day in receiving calls, setting off my visitors at several different times, and providing refreshments—it entirely accords with my disposition. . .to extend to my beloved friends a full measure of kindness and hospitality, and should it not be permitted that I live to repeat similar attentions, I may record that I have comfort in having hitherto done what I could . . .

Tues Apr 11th I have added a note to the memoranda for the executors of my Will, proposing that they shall endow the almshouses my dear and honoured mother built for four widows, that a sum be invested which shall yield 4s weekly to the said widows. This settlement seems entirely due from me, etc.

Tues. Apr 18th This morning received the intelligence of dear John Henry [Pease] having departed this life about 2 o' clock yesterday, at Clifton; his end was peaceful, and with a blessed hope, as would appear

from answers to questions. . .This is our monthly meeting day at Staindrop. I was most easy to stay at home with Charles and Francis Richard John Henry's brothers] who are now my inmates. Jos. Whitwell and Edward [two more brothers] will join us at dinner . . .
Joseph and Emma returns from Clifton, bringing lifeless John Henry with them, another interesting and lovely branch left from the parent stock.

Sun Apr 23rd The interment. . .of my dear Grandson John Henry took place at half past ten. The attendance was very numerous. The meeting was a very quiet and I trust a very instructive one . . .My dear John ministered. In the evening about seventy friends, relations, and young men of John Henry's acquaintance assembled, and the evening seriously and becomingly spent.
Thursday, 4th He travels to London with Joseph and Emma and his own servant, "Charles"—Our train, thirty or more carriages with two locomotives, travelled the 240 miles without one minute's delay from an accident, so marvellously complete is mechanical power and arrangement. . .
He travels to Birmingham on the 7th Aug., to the funeral of "dear Cousin Rachel Lloyd," and on the day of the funeral, he remarks on the large number present; 100 relations assemble in the evening. The following day he travels to London and stays at Tottenham with Josiah Forster, and on the 10th. Goes to Walden, till the 18th and so home in good health.

Tues May 23rd Showery, fine weather, bearing the promise of a fruitful year. Grain has been advancing in price from the devastation of foreign exporting ports, and the wicked waste of a wicked and cruel war.
On the 31st he enters his eighty-eighth year.
An important interesting day of many considerations, retrospective, present, and prospective. Surely a life so prolonged ought to have yielded more fruit . . .
He gets very anxious about his grandson.
Dear J.W.P. thin and not quite so well. Sometimes my fears are quickened respecting him in the thought that he has never looked so well since a violent fall in the stable yard of Edmund Backhouse's, at Middleton (Lodge).

On the 7th June—Very thoughtful in the night about my beloved Grandson, Jos. W. Pease, seeing him look so thin and delicate yesterday. Should it be in the Counsel of the Omnipotent Will that he should be taken, (but O, that it may not be so) what a dissolution of flattering prospects as to this world, to himself and all his family and to me during my remaining short life! . . .Some feelings in my heart, perhaps nervous, have awakened seriousness.

Fri June.23rd My dear Joseph and Emma got home this forenoon. I am comforted in seeing them look so well after the toil and tugging arising from having to defend the Bills IN Parliament, which he and his associates did successfully—The Barnard Castle Railway—The S.& D. Junction from St. Helens to the Tunnel, and the Tees Conservancy.

He finds that, as always is the case, the endeavours to serve friends needs the sacrifice of time and trouble, and the "constant engagement with visitors and friends deprives of time for mental introversion," and adds—you must both time and money spend to lay an obligation on a friend.

Sat June 22nd Marske. To the Ironstone diggings, with upwards of twenty sons, daughters, grandchildren and servants. The day was beautiful, the elevated mountain scenery very interesting, the toil of cart travelling over rough or constructed roads rather fatiguing but the enjoyment outweighed. The digging for ore and the superincumbent soil also beyond expectations, it is apprehended will arise.

Fri Aug 4th A very full town on account of a floral and agricultural Show; the former of these, in my apprehension, has an excess of vanity and expenditure in it, which I doubt a most tender conscience, feeling to the full the distresses and wants of the poor, could not allow themselves to indulge in. I condemn no man, but happy is the man of tender conscience that does not condemn him in the thing that he allows.

Aug. 7th Observed with grateful joy a fine field of very fine thick standing wheat, looking as if the sickle might soon entreat.

Aug.9th—To-moro my Bees go to the moors as annually.

Aug.11th—Observed a field of Barley cut near Marske, the first one this season.

On the 19th Finds him in Scotland.

Sat Aug19th Aberdeen. Reached this place this evening and in time to attend the meeting for ministers and elders; present, Anthony Wigham, Lydia Barclay, etc.

He sticks to his duty in Scotland, and thereby gives up the pleasure of being at his eldest grandson Joseph Whitwell Pease's, wedding. On Saturday, 26th August, he says: "in some respects it has been an important week to my precious family. Dear Joseph W. Pease's marriage with Mary Fox. My mind often visited them, their beloved parents and the family;

my desire and trust is that this union has the divine sanction, and will be blest."

Fri. Sept 1st Purchased a house on Cleveland Terrace (£400) that I might accommodate Ann Elizabeth Dale. Went to Stapleton to see Christopher Johnson, reduced weak, and feeble . . .The season continues most beautiful, near Cleasby, several stacks of wheat. The Cholera yet continues in Middlesboro'. My son and daughter Gibson and daughter left me for Balder Grange.

Fri. Sept. 15th . . . The day of the Flower show, a matter in which I take no further interest than to encourage the Cottagers to cultivate gardens for useful vegetables, or to keep bees. . . . .Mine is permitted for years past to be a calm, peaceful descent to a similar narrow cell where my dearest is laid, after, may my god grant my spirit be where hers is. .

Wed. Oct 4th —Early part of the day much occupied with callers whom I had not seen before . . .The after part of the day it was grateful employ to have to celebrate my Loved Grandson J.W.P.'s marriage by a bride's visit.

A day of rejoicing to many, and of mourning, I hope, to many on account of the intelligence of the taking of Sabastopol. The carnage and consequent misery deplorable; probably more than 20,000 killed and wounded, Russians and allies. . .

Sat Oct 7th . . .Accounts are received of a most alarming destruction by a conflagration having taken place at Gateshead and Newcastle by the explosion of several tons of gunpowder, brimstone, etc., very many houses burnt down, the glass in hundreds of houses broken, many lives lost, and the infirmary filled with those who are injured [He sends £20 for the relief of suffers] Dalias all killed by frost.

Tues Oct 10th—The accounts from the seat of war are of dreadful slaughter of English, French and Russians near Sabastopol, and the aqueducts to that city being cut off I fear an intense and wasting misery to the innocent and all inhabitants is bitterly felt. Oh for the Reign of the Price of Peace.

Fri Oct 13th—Received an account of the loss of the Arctic, on board of which were upwards of 300 persons, only about 50 saved. On board this vessel, an American steamer, was my dear friend Mahlon Day, his wife and daughter, so recently, so very agreeably with me. His loss will be lamented and keenly felt by the Friends of New York, of which meeting he was a truly valuable member. A mournful calamity permitted by infinite goodness.

Fri.Oct.20th—S. Smiles was with me to obtain particulars for a memoir of the life of George Stephenson. It appears to me that Railways will be a favour to the World, and I do not regret, but far otherwise, that my time, care and attention was so closely occupied for many months. Except with the help of a faithful secretary, R. Oxley, the care and charge of providing all materials and all the costs for the Waymen's wages rested on me. If I have in anyway made a humble instrument of use in the creation, all the praise, and I render it, is due to my God.

Sat Oct 21st—A tendering sweet feeling of being united to my precious ones gone before into the Realms of Joy and peace, my treasures already there. The blessings of my existence, my precious wife, my daughter Mary, my son Isaac, my son Edward, my daughter Rachel. Sweet affectionate, obedient, loving, pious children.

Mon Oct.23rd—My friend, Robert Stephenson the engineer, to spend two or three days with me—a man of most highly gifted and talented power of mind, of benevolent, liberal, kindly, just, generous dispositions, in company most interesting. My dear sons John and Henry dined with me At tea at my son Joseph's, a considerable and interesting company. At home to sup, and after it some social interesting subject occupied us to near eleven.

Tues Oct 24th—At breakfast with dear Henry; present, Robert Stephenson, John Dixon, T. McNay, F. Mewburn, David Dale, Beaumont Pease, J. Pryor Hack, and Thomas Booch. After breakfast, Robert Stephenson and four more went up the S & D line as far as Hounds Gill, and enjoyed their day. The evening pleasantly spent nearly alone, expressing to Robert Stephenson my anxious desire that smoking and taking wine might be carefully limited, free open converse, Oh my soul, be upon the watch. . .

Thurs Oct 26th—Robert Stephenson, after a pleasant social visit, left me this morning . . .

Fri. Oct 27th . . .In the evening I had the company of the three sisters Procter and twenty of their pupils. To entertain them and see them in pleasant health and spirits is very grateful to my mind. A present of a book was made to each girl.

Mon Nov 6th—Affecting account of misery in Sabastopol, and devastation of the bombarded City; the cruel want of water, the misery and wretched state of the English soldiers by the want, it may be said, of efforts to make existence anything but one of great privation and distress, and among my countrymen added to their misery great numbers slaughtered and far more suffering by wounds. When shall horrors cease ? May the Highest hasten the day.

Fri.Nov.17th—Wrote to E.P. Gurney. Is the sword, so destructive in this sad war, to devour forever ? Surely in the favoured but lowly and despised Society of Friends that day which is foretold of bending the sword into a ploughshare has dawned. Oh, that the accomplishment of this prophesy might soon be fulfilled, that the earth might enjoy its Sabbath

Sat.Nov.18th. . .Accounts of great slaughter among the troops in the Crimea; very many of the finest men in the English Army, the Guards.

Mon.Nov.20th—There is at this time great exertions making in every part of the Kingdom to raise a very large sum called a Patriotic Fund, for the widows and orphans of those who may be slain in battle or die of disease in the Crimea or elsewhere. In this movement friends feel they can take no share or mix themselves in anything connected with war, yet if poor sufferers come under their notice the law of kindness must be fulfilled.

Wed.Nov.29th—The £500 we [Robert Stephenson & Co.] have given for the establishment of schools at Newcastle on the broadest and most tolerant religious principles, seems to me will be got hold of by the never satisfied grasp of the Church of England,--doomed some day, I do believe, to melt away, it may be political strife; but a day of more light and truth will follow.

Wed.Dec.13th—Accounts from that scene of bloody warfare are on every ground discouraging and very affecting. Sufferings and slaughter very great. Parliament met yesterday, and I am sorry to observe, however angrily anyone may speak of the neglect of many essential things, a warlike spirit prevails in the nation. Oh my soul, be mindful and careful about thy own business.

Mon.Dec.25th—This day having a popish designation, Christ's Mass, may well be thankfully remembered by the pious Christian, if it is the day on which the Saviour of men was ushered into the world gladdening good old Simeon and everyone in measure who rightly thinks of this great event—but to what an extent this day is spent in riotous banqueting and forgetfulness !

The following day he entertains all his descendants about Darlington and others, "twenty one in all." On the 30th December, he records, "The first Iron Drawn from the two newly erected furnaces." This was the birth of the Great Cleveland iron trade.
Considering his soul's progress during the year, he puts certain queries to himself, and in "great reverence and humility,"can say that he trusts he is nearer" in preparation and fitness" for his change.

The love of my Lord and the more constant sense of his presence and overshadowing abiding with me, being more preciously as well as more generally felt, with supplication for complete purity and sanctification

Year 1855

From now until the end of 1857 the writing gets gradually more shaky, but it is easily read. There is hope in his religious entries, and he has a keen eye for Nature and agriculture still. Has problems keeping awake at meetings, and remembers his wife regularly. He travels to meet relations and Friends, and calls at Ayton to monitor the progress of the Agricultural School. He mentions the signs of old age "some feelings of trembling in walking," and a tendency to stagger in stepping."

Tues.Jan. 9th Cheering tidings of peace being near are currently believed. He refers in January to the pleasure of his visits to Woodlands, to see his grandson "J.W.P. and his Mary." And throughout the year continues a habit of spending every" seventh-day evening"with his" beloved descendants" at Southend. With his usual hospitality his house seems to be generally full of visitors. In regard to one party of relations from a distance who settled down on him he makes the only remark that betrays that he is ever tried by the continual arrivals and departures of the guests, and is rather a good one:
While I feel thankful for being enabled to exercise a kind hospitality to my friends and relatives, yet the social comfort varies greatly between those who come to partake and share the enjoyment of pure friendship and those who come solely for their own convenience, it is a difference between a sacrifice that costs something and enjoyment.

On the 17th He says there are no more tidings of the approach of the blessing of peace, but thinks apparently the fall in the price of wheat 6s. per quarter in London, a good sign and "a cheering change for the poor."

Wed.Jan. 31st—Great political changes anticipated by Lord

John, Russell's resignation. Ministry outvoted by 257 majority. To me it appears gloom is continually spreading over the prospects of this Kingdom, and it may be in the Counsel of infinite wisdom that ere the troubles of Europe and this wicked war cease, that the great parent of all who once said, "I will overturn—I will overturn," may execute the like sentence on this and other lands

Tues.Feb.6th—Received an account of the death of my cousin William Aldam, the only surviving descendant of my uncle Thomas Pease. W.A.'s character as a very honourable merchant and man stood high, with good dispositions and kindness without a (very) tender conscientious attachment to the principles of Friends, it may be said he walked with them . . .
He is glad that it was in the hearts of his dear sons "to give half-a-ton of coal to the innumerable poor widows and families" this month. He refers at times to the war, but sees "little abatement in the sad infatuated spirit which has so lamentably prevailed," and remarks that "confusion seems to stand at the door of all War proceedings abroad, and in all legislative proceedings at home. The last four weeks has seen Lord Aberdeen's ministry quite overturned; Lord Palmerston formed a new one, it soon dislocated itself and again for a week or two we were without a Government."

Sat. Feb.24th—Lord J. Russell gone to Vienna to endeavour to make peace. May he be able to effect a measure which seems fraught with so many blessings to the greatly misguided country. John Bright, with a temperate manly boldness, expresses his earnest sentiments on the war and all the measures of Government. It appears to me he is teaching Parliament and men in power more correctly to act, to think, and to speak, and that there is truth of great utility generally in his declarations.
He alludes on the 5th March to the death of the Emperor of Russia, and hopes peace may be among the changes caused by the event.

Wed. Mar 4th—Went with dear John to call on Henry Paskoe Smith, at Hall Garth, a worthy Magistrate, and very useful in this vicinity. H.P. Smith is a man of buoyant spirits and uncommonly facetious, with good sense. Apprehending a day of solemn consideration through divine mercy might yet be his, in a few words I adverted to it and gave him J. J. Gurney's valuable work on love to god. Do I sufficiently love God?

Fri.Mar23rd—Government having ordered that no interments shall take place in our

burying ground nearer than twenty feet of the Meeting-house, or any other dwelling house, I have planted Lauristinus, Box, and Chinese Arborvitae, near the Meeting House, and a yew hedge across the burying ground at the west end of the Meeting-House.
Edward remarks that this day, Friday 6th April, being Good Friday, is a Popish Mass day, and everyone in Darlington is idle.

Mon. Apr 16th—Beautiful mild weather, heavenly good-ness allows all round me that is visible to smile. But, oh for this poor sinful kingdom, while destruction and horrid slaughter is going on by the fierce bombardment of Sebastopol, by the English and French, the Sovereigns of both are now revelling in the waste and splendour of our national resources in London. Surely the Most High will be avenged if such doings and such a nation as this, etc.

Thurs.Apr19th—At Ayton to attend the interment of worthy Hannah White, the once faithful nurse of my beloved Mother and sister Mary until the close of their days. She was two years younger than myself. . .
War—All yet seems dark; it may be that this transgressing Kingdom may have to feel that which is reported regarding Russia, the revolt of the Serfs against the Nobles. . .The Emperor of the French has had two pistol shots aimed at him.
He goes to Hartlepool early in June to see Cuthbert Wigham, "a sweet character," and on to Seaton" to see the meeting house and little property thereto." He is thoughtful about his son Joseph's name being brought before the meeting as suitable for the station of elder."On the 31st May he completes the eighty-eighth and enters his eighty-ninth year of his pilgrimage in this vale of vicissitudes." He makes this month his annual balance" of his accounts and from the advance in value of Railway shares, discovers "a large increase of his property," and prays he may dispose of it in useful gifts and almsgiving, for all my Lord gives, it is yet his own, and oh that he may condescend to instruct in all respects of its use.

Sat. July.21st—For the last two weeks I have found my walking powers diminish so that to walk hence round the orchard requires two or three rests, but how gently and kindly my Heavenly Father deals with me in leading me through life . . .
He notes. . .for weeks past rain has fallen that I do not remember equally destructive hay weather—in many places it has been gathered to the dunghill instead of the stack.
On Friday 10th August, he goes to Newcastle, and has an "agreeable meeting" with

"Robert Stephenson respecting admitting W. Weelans into partnership in the Forth Street

concern," and stays at "cousin Geo. Richardson's, much to my comfort." He stays at Marske, where Joseph's seaside residence, Cliff House, still meets with some disapproval the following day he visits Hutton Low Cross, where his grandson, J.W.P. has his shooting, and stays in the Autumn.

Wed.Aug 22nd—Accounts of great slaughter of the poor Russians in the Crimea, 4000, or 5,000 ! Surely the wickedness of this country is great in not insisting on our Government to make peace, and how increased is the wickedness of this Kingdom in hiring the innocent Swiss, Germans, and Sardinians to fight in the Crimea. If National crimes are to be repaired by National punishments, heavy is the scourge we may receive, but man's great transgressions are oft passed over by gracious God, whose mercy is greater.
News from Sabastopol is a description more horribly wicked and cruel than I believe History has ever told: the burning of a hospital with 1,000 wounded soldiers raving mad with thirst and agony.

Fri. Oct 19th—A beautiful fine mild day, after a severe frost two or three days ago which killed the dahlias, etc. Fruit exceedingly abundant. 'Apples, Pears, and Plums very cheap, potatoes good and very little disease but very high priced, 2/9d per bushel. Wheat 10/6d, Oats 4s bushel. Monetary matters in France and England much convulsed discounts now seven per-cent.
Among Edward's visitors for this month are Lord Henry and Lady Vane; he talks with these for over two hours, saying "she is an agreeable woman and he an intelligent well informed man.

Wed. Dec 28th—Burning letters and papers that my dear executors might have less to do when the solemn duty falls upon them which has occupied much of my time and attention. My hope is that they will find very few of my accounts troublesome or intricate.

Fri.Dec.28th—At Southend. The evening spent less to my comfort than usually, the levity etc., of what is termed a Christmas Tree was below that which belongs to those who have attained to matured years.
He reviews the year including his own good health and also the good health of his precious descendants adding Surely I must be drawing near the end of my long life. May he condescend to be with me at the most awful hour . . .and in mercy, all of mercy, receive me into his heavenly Garner—Amen.

Year1856

On the fly-leaf of his diary is written, "Often and much alone, this book may be called my communing Companion."
He begins the year by wanting as usual to go to Newcastle to the Quarterly Meeting, but feels it will be too much for him. He comforts himself that eighteen of his family go. He enjoys entertaining relations, and having letters read out to him, which his dear departed mother wrote, when in her eightieth year the same day he hears some cheering news that the basis of peace has been agreed on.

Fri.Jan.22nd—Very thoughtful in hearing my dear son Henry was contemplating a trans-Atlantic tour, affectionately depending on my conclusion. May we be assisted to determine aright.

Wed. Mar.5th—Burning a great number of letters from my beloved sons and daughters and grandchildren. All proofs of their most comforting kindness and affection are strongly expressive of this and many matters and thoughts of enduring interest.
He enjoys having thirteen of his grandchildren with him, and in a beautiful sort of prayer for their future ends, "may we love him to the end: then he will love us to the end."

Sat Mar.15th—I was brought very low on hearing that an association of young Friends at Bradford had agreed to give the use of simple language. I lament it; Is not this a time which we may as of old say the Tents of Cushan are in affliction. Is not such combination comparable in disposition to those who formerly broke down the carved work of the Lord's house with axes and hammers.

He goes to sit by his "dear sinking Anna's" death bed; it reminds him of the days when he sat by the "same bed when my dear languishing brother [Joseph Pease, of Feethams] was laid thereon." She dies on the 2nd of April. It is curious to note his pleasure in simple things: he attends "an interesting lecture on geology. He still watches his garden: notes when the first asparagus is cut (26th April), when the gooseberries set, when the Lilacs come into leaf and are "showing for flower," and when the plum and Jargonelle trees are in blossom. He never forgets his lost Rachel, and says, "If it is permissible to enjoy that which is not revealed and is hidden; then he may note the sweet, indescribable sense of endearment which visits his spirit when he thinks of his precious one in bliss and his beloved children, loved all far beyond all words can tell."

Wed. Apr.30th—At Southend with the Trustees of Thomas Richardson's Legacy Fund, dear Henry and Samuel Gurney not present. It was a pleasure to see the distribution of many donations. . . encouragement for pupil teachers, Friends in low circumstances, for schools, and the blind such as I apprehend would be approved had T.R. been living.

Sat. May.17th – In looking to spend the afternoon with my seven grandchildren at Southend (their parents being in London) I compare myself to the stem of an old rough barked Oak quite staghorny in its branches, with a few greeh worn leaves upon them, incapable of being to them what I would, a gratefully refreshing shade.

Wed. May.21st—Swallows first noticed this season.

Fri., May., 30th –My health is all personal feeling is perfect. Stiffness of limbs, limited power of action and walking more completely confirm my old age than any other senses. Sight is imperfect, taste, touch feeling and hearing unimpaired. Great is the longing of my soul to return to my gracious creator, thanks and praises due.
The next day he notes, "This my Natal day, entering my ninetieth year."

Sunday 8th June, he "heard of the death of dear Sam. Gurney, at Paris," and the next morning writes:
"On reflecting on beloved Sam. Gurney, I see the man beyond all others I ever knew, the accumulator of vast wealth, in talent conspicuously pre-eminent, kind, generous, beloved, a Friend sound in principle, bound to the Society, in candour and counsel remarkable. In the meeting for Sufferings I have admired his clear directing views, and also in our Yearly Meetings often dropping wise, just, good opinions. His end was in blessed peace."
On the 10th He goes with about fifty young people and others "to Hutton Ironstone Diggings. Delighted with the mountainous scenery, and dining on the heather covered hills under a wall; then to Cleveland Lodge and a bountiful tea on the lawn in front of the house." On the 14th He adds:
Joseph left home to attend the burial of Sam. Gurney's remains, and this forenoon the mourners (very sincere ones they will be) may be standing round the grave of this almost unequaled man.
Wed.July.9th—The Barnard Castle Railway was opened yesterday; it was wet.
On the 17th "got up all my hay in good condition. Little of Summer warmth has yet been felt, and very late are all the products of the earth; and on the 22nd the first hot day this

season". He spends it in, "tranquil delight." Seated with his grandchildren "on the terrace at Marske," and adds, just like himself, "I fear my mind was more at ease and peace from my nature rather than of grace." On the 29th he dines with 130 at the annual school meeting at Ayton.
On the first August Friday, went up the Barnard Castle Railway with my dear son Joseph. The day very warm but no change of colour, as of approaching harvest, yet perceptible.
In the evenings of these hot days he drives out and records the appearance of crops, and the first "harvest tints in the cornfields." On considering all he has given away to his family and sons, he looks forward to being rather straightened and limited in my annual income. He says "I am now much alone, except when my dear grandsons come in to dine," all the family being away at Marske and Ayton. It is not till the 20th of August that he first can record corn cut. "Two fields of Barley cut near Gainford; the price of grain rises."

Fri. 22 August.—My cousin J. B. Braithwaite, his Martha, sister, nurse and three children came, their company pleasant and instructive. As Friends in consistent principles and demeanour truly exemplary, it is a comfort to see and entertain such strangers.
On the 2nd September he is "informed that my beloved Elizabeth Lucy was yielding to John F.; she is a lovely, sweet child." John Fowler whom she married, was the inventor of the steam plough; he died from the results of a hunting accident, when I was a small boy, and the big weight-carrying grey horse that fell with him was at our stables after the accident, at Hutton. When my uncle John died, my father ordered the horse to be shot, and I went to say goodbye to him as he stood with his head over the gate of a paddock before he was executed. I can remember my indignation at the deed, and my thoughts as I saw his limbs hanging in the kennel larder, and my disgust at being told his skin would fetch ten shilling or a pound. John Fowler left one son, John Ernest, who died at Algiers at the age of twenty one.

Fri.Dec.12th—Much converse about a railway to Kendal, etc., Henry at Ulverstone respecting it. . .

Mon. Dec.22nd—Two of the girls from the Proctors' Boarding School, Mary Allan and Webb, from Mullen, are with me during the major part of their vacation.

Sat. Dec.27th—At Southend, and the two Irish girls, Webb and Allan, now with me. The Emperor of Russia has signified that he designs to admit a Constitution to the Finns, treated to so much cruelty by the Baltic

Fleet. Friends have ever been against war and piracy.

Wed. Dec.31st . . .The past year and bygone years have found me, especially since my precious companion was taken to heaven, more and more anxious to aquatint myself with God, who in His great mercy has condescended to draw near to me, visited me in His love and granted me, blessed for ever be His Holy name, a good hope that through the intercession and advocacy of His Son, who laid down his life for my complete redemption, I may be an heir of Immortality in his kingdom. I should be short of that gratitude which is due to my gracious Creator if I do not commemorate the past year as one of abounding mercy every way. The blessings of a happy and entirely healthy existence. . .surrounded by descendants of three generations. . . .all having my prayers that they may be more faithful and far more useful in their generation. . .What the unfolding of the coming year may be is known only to Him who doeth all things right and well. AE. 89 and 7 month.

Year 1857

This is the last year of the Diaries, the writing becomes more shaky, eyes dim with age. A slip is found in this volume—*These books, kept for a notice of passing events and often giving rise to a self review and seriously useful reflections, sometimes personnel.*

Sat. Jan.17th—A subject of general converse and greatly condemned is the Bombardment of Canton; the destruction of the City and Forts is deemed a harsh and cruel revenge for some misdoing of the Governor . . .
He alludes with gratification to the proposed "railway across the Kingdom to unite this county with Westmoreland and Lancashire," but has no desire to live to see this and many other works of utility accomplished.

Sat Feb.7th—Heard of the decease of my cousin George Stacey in the evening of the last 5th day. Years have passed over since his powers of mind and body were almost entirely (the latter especially) prostrated. In middle life he was an active and truly valuable member of our Society, for several years Clerk to the London Yearly Meeting.

Wed. Mar.4th—The news this morning is very interesting and acceptable. The House of Commons have condemned that province which the Ministry has given to the cruel bombardment of Canton—majority against Lord Palmerston sixteen. In the House of Lords the conduct of Sir John Bowring and Admiral Seymour was approved, and nine Bishops voted in favour of this cruelty and bloodshed!

SatMar7th—I find the conclusion of a public town meeting is to grant my earnest request that no Testimonial be presented to me on account of my persevering efforts to perfect the first public Railway ever thought of. In this undertaking I had a good helper and warm coadjutor in my cousin Jonathon Backhouse, yet his cares and attention were much more remitting (sic) than mine.

Mon. Mar.23rd—A day of some trouble and anxious care, for my beloved Henry having consented to offer himself as a candidate for South Durham, has issued his address and is to expose his political opinions, etc., etc., before the assembled freeholders this evening. He has my near and very affectionate sympathy in this great voluntary trial he has brought upon himself. I think he will not be disappointed; if he is, I am ready to believe it may be a blessing for him . . .

Fri.Mar.27th—The day of Caroline Doyle's interment at Bristol, a day of mourning for the families of Fry. Dear Henry with his brother Joseph at the Hartlepool's to day. I am anxious about their reception there, prejudiced as the people of West Hartlepool are by Ward Jackson, a bottomless man.
The next day at Southend he finds his "cheerful grandsons greatly interested and bustling about their Uncle Henry's election."

Fri April3rd—The Parliamentary struggle was over this evening. Pease 2,568, Vane 2,533, Farrar 2,089. This result proves this section of the Country is not in the dictation of the Duke of Cleveland. Yet the decision as regards my precious son yields me no comfort, my fears and foreboding are in some degree those of apprehension that it will not be for his soul's peace or that this dear son may be exposed to temptations and discomforts . . .
He himself remains "thankfully free from every excitement as regards the result."

Mon.April 6th—Considerable excitement in the town, the Sheriff declaring the election of Pease and Vane. My mind does not derive comfort from dear Henry's election, but as an increase of virtuous right-minded men in the House of Commons is greatly to be desired, so I desire that merciful overruling goodness may permit some enduring good to spring out of what my dear son does consider to be his right and important station.

Fri.Apr.24th—My friend Robert Stephenson came in about noon, he accompanied me to my nephew John B.P. to meet all my sons, daughters and their descendants in this place who were present. The evening was pleasantly and gratifyingly spent in converse. But oh, my leanness in feeling at home in the body . .

Sat.Apr.25th—R. Stephenson left this forenoon; his representation of the Forth Street concern bright and encouraging. He handed a Hitching Railway bond to the amount of £5,000 for dear Joseph and myself; the bonds are at par, being four per cent. Bonds. Cold.

Mon.Apr.27th—A pleasant assemblage at my dear Grandson J.W.P., and his Mary and her sister, socially, I hope allowably spent. . .

Wed. Apr.29th—Prolonged and how long has been my voyage on this boundless ocean of time, how large and manifold have been my blessings and preservations through the unmerited mercy of God. Ah, and how have I seen them that had forsaken Him blasted and blighted and obviously sink, whilst those that live near to the blessed instruction of his Spirit had in all respects a prosperous voyage and at last anchored where there were no more storms.
On the 1st May Henry joins him at breakfast, "having yesterday taken his seat and been present at the choice of Speaker, etc., and returns home for the weeks recess."

Fri. May.8th—Planted the West yard of the Meeting-house with cuttings of Ivy with the expectation that some day(not one that I shall live to see) It will be clothed with green and add to the agreeable appearance of the Grave Yard. My beloved daughter Gibson and her Francis came this evening, much to my comfort.
They leave on the 19th And he settles in at Southend.

Tues.June.2nd—Deprived as I am of the power of reading the Holy Scriptures except the Book of Psalms, and the New Testament which I greatly value, as having these in large type, I often lament that my memory does not supply me with recollection of a larger number of instructive passages from the bible.

Mon.June.29th—My dear Grandson Joseph W.P. announces to me that this morning a son is born to him. It interests me to have a male representative of my family in the third generation. May he, like Samuel, if favoured to live, be a blessing and comfort to his parents. May they dedicate him to the Lord and train him for a dedication so Holy!
He goes to Ayton even though he is now ninety, and even attends the general meeting there, "Accompanied by Lucy Fowler and Wm. Ball; 120 dined at the school" (4th August).

Thurs.Aug.6th—This day the marriage of my beloved Grand-daughter Elizabeth Lucy, to John Fowler. The meeting very large – The ministry of John Dodshon, John Pease and the supplication of Isaac Sharp . . . pertinent to the occasion and instructive.
He records the death of Thomas James Backhouse at Seaton. He goes to Barnard Castle with Rachel Fowler, and throughout the autumn makes his observations on the crops and weather, as of old

Fri Sept.18th. . . Accounts are still received from India of fresh revolts and sad details of most cruel murders of hundreds of men, woman and children, of officers and civilians, that hundreds of Europeans have fallen before a savage, infuriated people and the rebellious Sepoys.

Sat Oct.3rd. . .While I think there is a Christian liberty as to the use of Liquor that can intoxicate, so I believe the Christian may use these liquors without abusing them or being abused by them. The Christian now, as the apostle formally, can do all through Christ strengthening him.

Wed.Oct.14th—Parted with dear, pious, intelligent cousin J. Bevan Braithwaite. His eye and intent seems whilst attending to claims upon him as a useful Barrister to be fixed on the business of his Lord and Master, his life and conduct is a lesson and teaching for me.

Thurs.Oct.15th—Informed of the death of my dear honoured valuable friend Sam Tuke, a man dignified by uncommon talents, most useful to the community and the church in writing, and otherwise accomplishing much. A course well run, a day's work well done. I seem to shrink into merely nothing when I look at the man, his work, and his worth and mine. . .Friend after Friend departs; surely I ought to consider the messenger at my door. How shall I feel on his arrival? I trust with a humble resigned spirit, with some blessed hope, some faith in divine mercy. . .There was a day when through infinite compassion in a time of great downbreaking it was given me to see that a door was open which no man should be able to shut, and whilst that doorway was narrow [writing here illegible].

Wed Oct 21—Great commercial difficulty and pecuniary distress is reported from America . . . Overtrading is the cause, so that nationally and individually it is true that they who make haste to be rich pierce themselves through with many sorrows.

Fri.Oct.23rd—Morning—I leave the record of this to me

eventful and rather trying day until it is closed. Noon. Called upon by twenty, mostly my fellow [townsmen?] to present me with an address commending my early exertions respecting Railways and Engineering, also my sons. While to be useful in our day and live in their esteem is to be gratified, yet the Address is quite too full and above all our services.

The Autumn is most "genial"; late in November there has been "no frost to injure the Dahlias and late flowers." He notes "the pecuniary troubles and difficulties which many opulent and highly respected houses are severely tried, and some compelled to close." He hears of relatives and Friends effected by this calamity, and is very much concerned, "especially for all those concerned pecuniary in the Shotley [?Shirley] Iron Works," and he does not see how they can "escape being swallowed in the Gulph." He attends regularly the "select meeting." On the 31st of December he makes a rather large entry, and says"

Winter has proceeded thus far without almost any appearance of it, the mildness, the aftermath of the day has been, and yet is quite remarkable; grass has continued to grow, and greenness is universal; primroses and similar evidences of spring from the swelled buds on the trees. . .

He mentions his descendants good health, and also the troubles regarding the failure of the Northumberland Bank. Then the last sentence of the records are as follows—Then as regards my precious Sons and Daughters , inexpressible is my comfort in them and in believing that the divine life within continues and does increase—weaning them from this perishable world.

His love of his family and friends marks him until the end. He lived until the end of July 1858, having loved God to the end, and who no doubt was with him at the end, and also, that he may be reconciled with his very precious Rachel in lasting peace.

The Clarence Railway
Robert Surtees

I gazed upon the low and quiet vale
Where Skerne slow wanders through the marshland green,
And lovely seem'd the tram-road dimly seen,
Breaking by fits the dull plantation's screen—
Whilst mov'd majestic, on the track of rail,
The steam-horse---clouds involve his haughty crest,
Whilst struggling sighs and flashing flames between,
Betray the fires that scorch his troubled breast.

Ah me! that thing so seeming-angel fair,
That glides along his own enchanted ground,
That treverses the fields like gentle air,
Diffusing Eden-odours all around,
Should in deep guile and malice so

Unaware,
Permits him pass his old paternal bound,
But treble woe to them who rear'd this black infernal mound!
Ah, little think the caitiffs as they wend,
Along destruction's slippery downward way,
To that grim shore their gliding railways tend—
How soon for them shall fade the golden day!

This Railway was planned very near to Mainsforth, and Surtees was opposed to the idea, but after it was re-routed he withdrew his opposition.

Backhouse Family,

The early Backhouse family were devout Quakers but as the years passed the activities of Edmund who was the oldest son of Sir Jonathan Backhouse changed the religious traditions of Quakers beyond belief; this was highlighted in Books 'A Hidden Life', & 'The Enigma of Sir Edmund Backhouse', both by Hugh Trevor-Roper. Edmund was recorded as a secret agent and even a Pornographer; he converted to 'Catholicism', later in his life. Two younger brothers attained high rank in the Royal Navy, when Roger finished his career as Admiral of the Fleet:

Bernie McCormick now retired spends his leisure hours reading and writing about Local History, Mining & also the wonderful characters, bred and born in our Islands, they contributed so much to the 'Whole World' in general; Bernie writes & self Publishers most of his own work he also enjoys Family History and has advised many on the techniques of Genealogy:

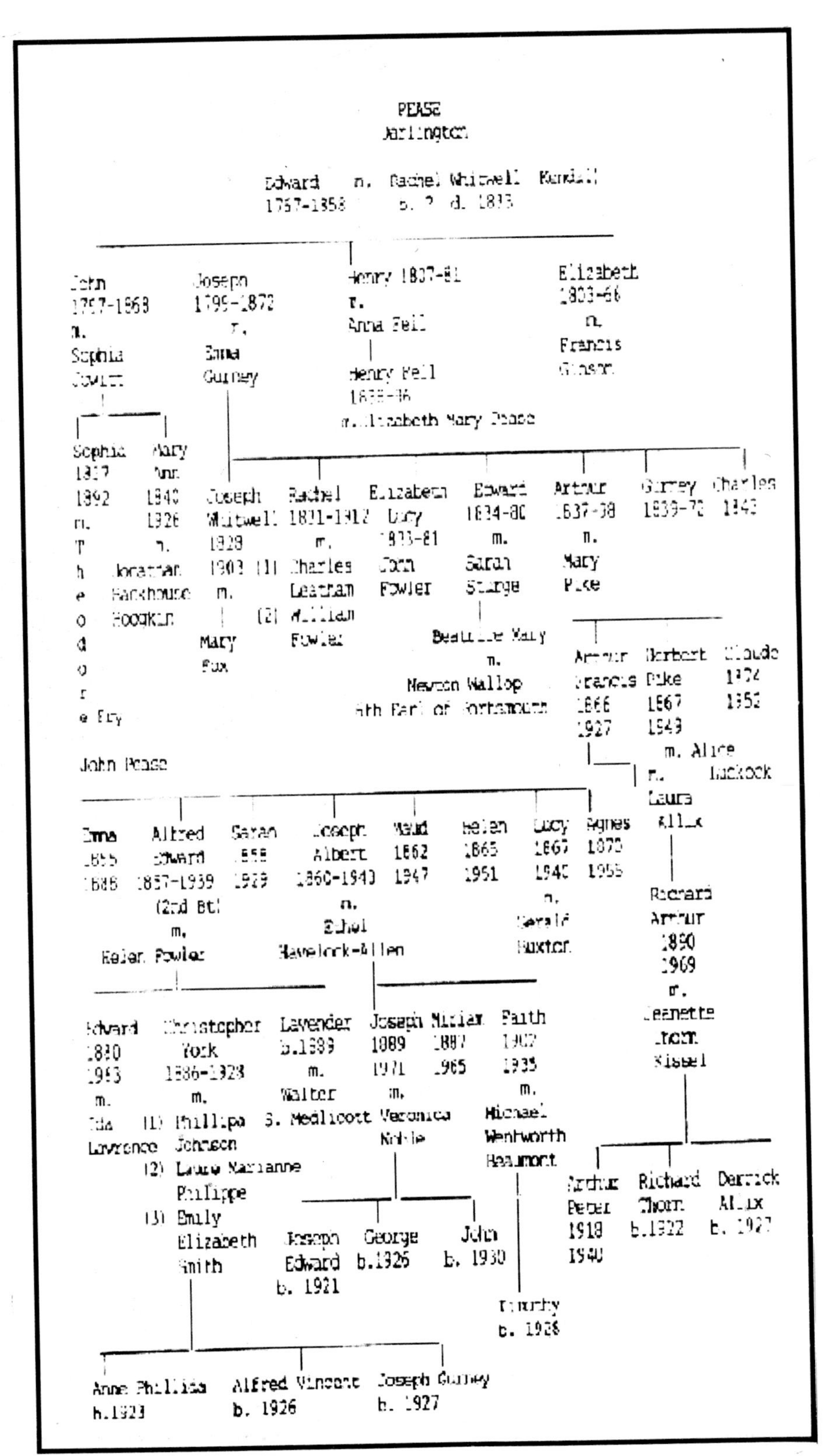
PEASE
Darlington
Edward m. Rachel Whitwell Kendall
1767-1858 b. ? d. 1833
John
1797-1868
m.
Sophia
Jowitt
Joseph
1799-1872
m.
Emma
Gurney
Henry 1807-81
m.
Anna Fell
Henry Fell
m. Elizabeth Mary Pease
Elizabeth
1808-66
m.
Francis
Gibson
Sophia
1817
1892
m.
Theodore Fry
Mary
Ann
1926
m.
Jonathan
Backhouse
Hodgkin
Joseph
Whitwell
1828
1903
m.
Mary
Fox
Rachel
1831-1912
m.
(1) Charles
Leatham
(2) William
Fowler
Elizabeth
Lucy
1833-81
John
Fowler
Edward
1834-80
m.
Sarah
Sturge
Arthur
1837-98
m.
Mary
Pike
Gurney
1839-72
Charles
1843
Beatrice Mary
m.
Newton Wallop
6th Earl of Portsmouth
Arthur
Francis
1866
1927
Herbert
Pike
1867
1949
m. Alice
Luckock
Claude
1874
1952
m.
Laura
Allix
John Pease
Emma
1855
1886
Alfred
Edward
1857-1939
(2nd Bt)
m.
Helen Fowler
Sarah
1858
1929
Joseph
Albert
1860-1940
m.
Ethel
Havelock-Allen
Maud
1862
1947
Helen
1865
1951
Lucy
1867
1940
m.
Gerald
Buxton
Agnes
1870
1955
Richard
Arthur
1890
1969
m.
Jeanette
Thorn
Kissel
Edward
1880
1963
m.
Ida
Lawrence
Christopher
York
1886-1928
m.
(1) Phillipa
Johnson
(2) Laura Marianne
Philippe
(3) Emily
Elizabeth
Smith
Lavender
b.1889
m.
Walter
S. Medlicott
Joseph
1889
1971
m.
Veronica
Noble
Miriam
1887
1965
Faith
1902
1935
m.
Michael
Wentworth
Beaumont
Arthur
Peter
1918
1940
Richard
Thorn
b.1922
Derrick
Allix
b. 1927
Joseph
Edward
b. 1921
George
b.1925
John
b. 1930
Timothy
b. 1928
Anne Phillida
b.1923
Alfred Vincent
b. 1926
Joseph Gurney
b. 1927

The 150th
ANNIVERSARY
1825 · 1975
STOCKTON
and
DARLINGTON
RAILWAY
Railway.
The Company's
COACH
EXPERIMENT;
10247295

INDEX

Gibson Francis 94,
Gibson P. 144
Girado Baron 117,
Gladstone 94,
Gloria Mundi 102,
Golightly Jane 21,
Gospel 117,
Government Legislature 145,
Gowland John 70,
Grand Jury 124,
Grantham 132,
Great North Road 57,
Gretna Green 11,
Grey Horse 36,
Guisborough 98, 125, 148,
Gurney Elizabeth 142,
Gurney Emma 88,
Gurney GP. 156,
Gurney Joseph 89,
Gurney Samuel 100, 161, 162,